Tracking Nana

By R.M. Hagan

ISBN: 978-0-578-57252-9

Albuquerque, New Mexico

Contents

1 EL VIEJO   5

2 "CAPTURE THESE DEVILS"   11

3 ACROSS THE RIO BRAVO   22

4 THE SACRED MOUNTAIN   43

5 PLÁCIDA'S SAD SONG   68

6 HOT PURSUIT   87

7 CUCHILLO NEGRO   98

8 AMBUSH IN GAVILAN CANYON   118

9 THE AFTERMATH   132

EPILOGUE   151

For maps and a hiking & camping guide to
Nana's Trail, see **trackingnana.com**

1

EL Viejo

"It is difficult to describe the horror and dismay which the names of the bloodthirsty and relentless Geronimo, Victorio and Nana struck to the hearts of the settlers of the Southwest in those days." – Col. George F. Hamilton[1]

Words have the power to shape the world around us. For the Apache, a man's true name was especially powerful, to be spoken only rarely when he was alive and never after his death. His people knew the old man as Kas-tziden *("Broken Foot")* for an old ankle injury that had never healed properly, or as Haškɛnadɨltla *("Angry, Agitated").* But for the Anglo or Hispanic tongue Apache names are almost impossible to pronounce correctly and even trickier to translate, so that most Apaches entered the historic record by Spanish or English nicknames – names like Delgadito *("Skinny")* and Cuchillo Negro *("Black Knife"),* or Deadshot and Skippy.

Nana's name may be a contraction of *"nantan,"* or leader, although he was never an elected chief like Cochise.[2]

---

[1] Schubert, Frank N. <u>Voices of the Buffalo Soldier.</u> .

Tracking Nana

No Apache called him "Broken Foot," a nickname that may be better translated as "Lame," to his face. He was no man to be defined by or even acknowledge his infirmities, and he bore the pain of his bad leg stoically, as he did the rheumatism that afflicted his later years. "He asked no odds because of either age or lameness," said his great-nephew James Kaywaykla, who as a little boy called the old man "grandfather."[3]

His other Apache name might be rendered in English as "Grumpy" or "Bad-tempered." He may have been a loveable grandfather to those around him, but in his best-known photograph he looks more like the "Hey, you kids! Get off my lawn!" type curmudgeon. In his case, the trespassing "kids" were the hairy, pale-eyed *gabachos* who suddenly showed up and started bossing people around like they owned the place when Nana was already approaching middle age.

Like many seniors, it made him angry to be treated like a child in his own home. When a portly young Army lieutenant presumed to instruct Nana and other chiefs on how to treat their wives, Nana abruptly stood up and told the interpreter: "Tell this fat boy I killed

---

[2] *While most sources render the old man's name as "Nana," a few spell the name with a tilde, as Naña, or with an "e" as Nane, and pronounce it with a heavy accent on the second syllable as Nanĕh.*

[3] Ball, Eve. In the Days of Victorio, U. of Arizona, 1970, p. 8

men while he was still in diapers! There's nothing he can teach me about women!" and stormed out.

Nana was born sometime before 1810 somewhere near the headwaters of the Gila River. He was a Chihenne (also Chihene, Chihende, Tcihene and other variations), the "red paint people," one of the four bands whites generally lumped together as the Chiricahua. (The Apache themselves considered only the neighboring Chokonen and Bedonkohe to be "true Chiricahua.") Although they ranged far south into Mexico, their homeland was centered around Ojo Caliente, their sacred warm spring in southwestern New Mexico. At one time or another Spaniards, Mexicans and Americans knew them as the Mimbres or Mimbreños (for the Mimbres River, which rises in what is today the Gila Wilderness), Copper Mines, Warm Springs or Ojo Caliente band.

Nana possessed two sources of supernatural help. The first was his Power over rattlesnakes. It's not clear whether he was able to cure snakebite or whether he could somehow control the snakes themselves. Either skill would have been highly respected by the Apache, who lived in a country where rattlers remain a danger today. The Apache reluctance to fight at night, disparaged by their white adversaries as the childish savage's superstitious fear of the dark, was at least in part a pragmatic estimate of the risks involved in crawling around in the brush after dark, when the reptiles were most active.

The association may also have conveyed a warning that he was a dangerous man to cross.

Nana's second gift was Power over ammunition, and he repeatedly led raids that captured guns and ammunition.[4] This Power would have grown in importance in the 1870's as Civil War-era guns (powder charge + bullet + percussion cap) wore out or broke and were replaced with cartridge arms (bullet, powder and cap all conveniently packaged in a metal case). The wide variety of calibers and powder charges for the available guns complicated the supply problem.

Whether armed with their favored Winchester repeaters or the Army's .45-70 Springfields, the hostiles found cartridges scarce in Mexico. As a result, the Apache committed a basic strategic error in waging war on both sides of the border. The Mexicans were a soft target, rich in horses and cattle, but it was necessary to raid into the United States to resupply ammunition. And despite long years of mutual hostility with the Mexicans, the Chiricahuas' basic grievance was the loss of their homeland in

---

[4] Sweeney, Edwin R. From Cochise to Geronimo; p. 168

Arizona and New Mexico to the encroaching Americans.

Pursued by both national governments acting in an uneasy commonality of interest, *los Indios bravos* ultimately found themselves without a safe sanctuary on either side of the line.

Nana was the uncle and right hand man of the great Victorio. At least one Army officer at the time believed Victorio *("the Winner")* owed much of his reputation for tactical genius to Nana, the canny veteran of years of raid and foray. Others credited Victorio's sister Lozen's uncanny ability to "see" the enemy from afar, sensing danger miles away. Certainly Victorio was without either of these trusted advisors when he made his final, fatal mistake.

As Victorio's s*egundo* (second in command) in the fall of 1880, Nana had the dangerous honor of commanding the rearguard as the band rode across the barren Chihuahuan desert below the *Rio Bravo*, probing for an unguarded ford that would allow them to cross the river and strike back north. As a result, Nana was miles away when the Mexicans trapped Victorio at Tres Castillos.

It's not hard to imagine the sick, sinking feeling the old man must have felt in the pit of his stomach when he heard gunfire not on his backtrail but from far ahead, where Victorio was leading the women and children to the little lake at Tres Castillos. With too few warriors to contest the Mexican force directly,

Nana tried to relieve the pressure on Victorio by lighting a brushfire in the hills to the south. He skirmished briefly with 30 Mexicans who were drawn off toward his fire, but the diversion was unsuccessful in breaking the ring trapping his chief.

The Mexicans credited a Tarahumara Indian with shooting Victorio dead and they presented the killer with a nickel-plated Winchester. The Apaches believed Victorio fought until he was out of ammunition and then killed himself with his own knife rather than be taken alive. Half the band died along with him and most of the survivors were herded off to Chihuahua City.

Only Nana and the warriors who had been with him, a few more who had been away from the main body on a separate raid for ammunition, and a handful of women and children who had somehow evaded their captors were left free. It was left to Nana to pick up the shattered pieces.

"We were too late," mourned one of the warriors who had been absent that terrible day, after surveying the bodies scattered among the barren rocks.

"It is not too late so long as one Apache lives," Nana responded.[5]

---

[5] Ball, <u>In the Days of Victorio</u>; p.101

2

"Capture These Devils"

"The Indian warfare as far as Victorio's band is concerned is ended, but we must not forget one principle of evolution, the survival of the fittest, the few that are left will be more treacherous, more ugly than ever before known." -- Grant County Herald, Oct. 1880[6]

Tres Castillos should have been so traumatic as to drive even the strongest man into a head-clutching, nearly catatonic fetal position, overwhelmed by the scope of the disaster. Instead, Nana acted quickly to gather the handful of survivors. According to Kaywaykla, a very young boy at the time, Nana led them west and then north across the border somewhere near the Arizona line, evading cavalry patrols to bring the little band back into their familiar New Mexico mountains.

It was cold in the high country that winter but safe enough, at least for the time being. The Texas cowboys and Hispanic *pastores* had driven their herds and flocks back down into the valleys, and the miners, prospectors and loggers were huddled in the bustling little camps that now fringed the mountains, waiting impatiently for the spring thaw to open up the canyons. In the meantime the hunting was

---

[6] Billington, Monroe Lee. New Mexico's Buffalo Soldiers, p. 97.

good, and the women made new moccasins and restocked the secret caches with food, spare blankets and – most important – ammunition. These hidden stockpiles were needed for the campaign Nana had probably begun planning even as he was shepherding the grieving survivors away from Tres Castillos.

Around the campfire at night, the old man told Kaywaykla tales out of the Apache mythic past, of Child of Waters and White Cloud Woman, heroes who dared fearsome perils and overcame great difficulties to save their People. "Grandfather impressed upon me that every struggle, whether won or lost, strengthens us for the next to come," Kaywaykla recalled many years later. "It is not good for people to have an easy life. They become weak and inefficient when they cease to struggle. Some need a series of defeats before developing the strength and courage to win a victory."[7]

As they traveled farther north through the ranch country near Horse Springs, Nana's impulsive young subordinate Kaytennae scooped up a little boy and a slightly older girl who were out herding cattle, riding double on one horse. Nana rebuked Kaytennae, telling him the two white children were useless and their loss was sure to put the cavalry on their trail. He told the younger man to get rid of his captives, and Kaytennae put them back on their horse and let them go after the band

---

[7] Ball, Days of Victorio, p.104.

moved on, according to what Kaywaykla's mother told him later.

Nana wanted to maintain a low profile not just because he was encumbered with women and children but because he had things to accomplish that winter. He was headed into the Mangas Mountains to make contact with kindred spirits.

There was trouble on the Navajo Reservation that year, where the *Diné* were so angry with their agent that he had found it prudent to move to Albuquerque and leave the military to deal with his unhappy charges. Some of the most restless of these were roaming the mountains south of the Zuni and Acoma reservations, and it was to them that Nana looked for allies. He also probably sent word east across the Rio Grande to where he still had friends among the Mescalero.

His preparations complete, Nana turned back south as the sun began its annual journey north. Late in the afternoon of Jan. 14, 1881, a band of Apaches attacked a wagon on the road 12 miles east of Fort Cummings, killing two men and perhaps abducting a woman whose shoes were found nearby. Two hours later, around sunset, the raiders ambushed a coach as it approached the stage station in the Good Sight Mountains, killing the driver, James Sweeney, and his passenger, Thomas White. The raiders cut open the mail sacks and scattered the contents, stole a shipment of musical instruments intended for the 12[8] Infantry band, and left their victims lying in the road, "their heads mutilated in a shocking manner."[8]

Lt. Col. Nathan Dudley, commanding at Fort Cummings and second in command of the 9th Cavalry, was so offended by these attacks that virtually the entire regiment was turned out "to capture these devils."[9]

Just who "these devils" were is something of a puzzle, however. There were said to be 40 or 50 of them, and their trail led north into the Black Range. A few days later, Indians jumped 9th Cavalry Lt. John F. McBlain, who was traveling in an Army ambulance on the wagon road that ran along the Rio Grande. The lieutenant and his driver escaped into the brush, but the Indians burned the wagon, killed one mule and wounded another, and stole the other two mules. Sometime after this, six Indians ambushed a stagecoach near Santa Barbara (today's Hatch), but were driven off by two soldiers riding the stage as guards.[10]

On Jan. 18, Apaches raided a little tent camp of 18 miners in Chloride Gulch, killed two men and drove off horses and mules. On Jan. 22, under the black headline **"Another Outrage,"** the *Albuquerque Journal* printed a telegraphic dispatch from Magdalena reporting that, "25 Indians have cleaned out Stapleton's

---

[8] *Albuquerque Daily Journal,* Jan. 18, 1881.
[9] Billington, pp. 101-2.
[10] ibid

Mill, 15 miles from this camp, committing murders, etc. Traveling northwest to Navajo Reservation." Three days later, headlined "Apaches Again," the *Journal* reported a Hispanic family – a man with two women and a boy – were "brutally murdered" by 26 Apaches on the road 15 miles southwest of San Marcial, near where Alamosa creek flows into the Rio Grande. The story went on to attribute to Captain Jack Crawford (a noted Indian scout then working as post sutler at Fort Craig) news that, "Mr. Robinson, mining engineer of the A.T.&S.F. was surrounded by the Indians and two of his men had been killed."

The *Santa Fe New Mexican* offered a slightly different and more detailed version of this event, reporting that mining engineer J.M.Robinson was traveling on a buckboard about five miles west of San Jose (on the Rio Grande where Elephant Butte Reservoir is now) at two o'clock in the afternoon of Jan. 23 when attacked. Robinson's driver and one horse were killed before the Indians drew off.

"The Indians surrounded a party consisting of three men and one woman, two miles west of the same point, on the same day. Robinson and seven Mexicans arrived on the scene in time to save the party. A fight took place, and Robinson and party were in danger of getting the worst of the affair, when five soldiers of Co. D, 9th Cavalry, who were escorting a contractor's train, came up and opened fire, driving off the Indians," the story continued.

Sgt. Madison Ingoman and six 9th Cavalry troopers were escorting a supply train along the Cañada Alamosa from Fort Craig to Ojo Caliente when they heard distant gunfire. Leaving the wagons corralled under protection of the teamsters, the sergeant took his little command to investigate. Finding seven civilians desperately defending themselves against 25 Indians, the soldiers charged to the rescue and drove the hostiles off. Two days later "still eight miles from Ojo Caliente," Pvt. William Jones was fatally wounded when Ingoman's train "was fired on by some fifteen Apaches positioned atop the canyon walls."[11]

Another, un-named source was cited for news that a band reported to number 54 Indians rode through the town of Hillsboro, firing into the houses as they passed, and on up into the Black Range, closely pursued by the soldiers. [12]

The scout Crawford was wounded on Jan. 31 when he and two civilian companions were attacked by five Apaches in the box canyon leading up to Ojo Caliente.[13] According to other reports the Indians stole two horses near Hillsboro and a buckboard near the little village of Cuchillo Negro, east of Chloride on the road to the Rio Grande.[14]

---

[11] Kenner, Charles L. Buffalo Soldiers and Officers of the Ninth Cavalry, 1867-1898, pp. 278-79.

[12] *Albuquerque Daily Journal*, Jan. 25, 1881.

[13] Kühn, Berndt. Chronicles of War, p.242.

[14] Billington, p. 101.

If all this violent activity seems confusing, that's perhaps because it was meant to be. Note too that all these incidents were east and south of Ojo Caliente toward the Rio Grande. The one exception, the report from Magdalena, proved to be inaccurate; the man said to be murdered at Stapleton's mill later turned up safe and sound, and Stapleton himself would later prove to be on friendly terms with the Apaches.

"After we turned south, Nana took half the warriors with him and put Blanco in command of the others who were to take the noncombatants to Sonora," Kaywaykla recalled many years later. "Our group went by Ojo Caliente, deserted by the soldiers. Blanco stationed guards to warn us of the approach of an enemy and for two days we stayed near the warm spring... We lay in the cleansing pool and enjoyed its beneficent effect for hours."[15]

After the Chihenne were rounded up and marched west to San Carlos in 1877, the abandoned Ojo Caliente agency intermittently served as a patrol base for the troops hunting Victorio from 1878-'80. That Sgt. Ingoman was delivering supplies there suggests the place was still occupied by troops that winter. If so, the choleric Col. Dudley's general alarm had sent them riding south in pursuit of the 12th Infantry's stolen band instruments before Blanco arrived at the spring.

---

[15] Ball, Days of Victorio, *p.108.*

Tracking Nana

It was likely Blanco and his sentries who killed Pvt. Jones and drove Sgt. Ingoman back out of the canyon that guards the eastern approach to the spring, while Nana himself led the earlier attacks farther toward the river.

But it's also possible Nana and his men were not responsible for all the depredation in the last weeks of January. Juh and Geronimo were both absent from their sub-agency in Arizona during this time period.[16] Although the agent claimed they remained someplace on the reservation, it could be they were the raiders who struck first in the Good Sight Mountains and then along the Rio Grande and up toward Hillsboro.

Whoever led the different parties, all these attacks were likely orchestrated by Nana to draw attention away from Blanco, who was escorting the women and children south. "Nana made a feint at attack to lure the cavalry toward the Floridas so that Blanco could take the emigrant wagon road west from the fort," Kaywaykla recalled. "He rode close enough to Fort Cummings to be sighted; then dashed toward the Floridas with the cavalry in pursuit."[17]

This ploy was only partially successful. Blanco stopped to water his horses at the spring virtually under the walls of the fort, then led the way west through Cooke's Canyon. But according to Kaywaykla, Blanco discovered a

---

[16] Sweeney, From Cochise to Geronimo, p. 168
[17] Ball, Days of Victorio, pp. 109-10.

force of cavalry following them down the trail; whether these troops were in pursuit of the Apaches or simply following the same road is unclear. Blanco ambushed the soldiers at a spring and killed several of their horses before they withdrew toward the fort, leaving two men behind on foot, and Blanco himself was killed before the Indians succeeded in killing those two troopers. Farther on, they discovered the western end of the main canyon was guarded and were forced to turn up a side canyon, where Blanco's brother Sudeen was killed in a skirmish that left three miners dead

I've seen no other account of these events, and Kaywaykla's description doesn't match the terrain in Cooke's Canyon. He was a little boy clinging to his mother at the time, and in recounting these memories 70 years later he may have conflated Cooke's with another canyon farther south. One compilation of 9th Cavalry actions lists a detachment of Co. K engaged in the "Candelaria Mountains, New Mexico" on Feb. 5, but the Candelarias are in Mexico southwest of Juarez, and I haven't seen any report of 9th Cavalry fatalities around this time.

Whatever the exact circumstances, the loss of two brave men was a severe blow to Nana. While the Army could count on a steady flow of recruits from the cities and farms back east, it took the Apaches 20 years to raise and train a warrior; his death was more than a personal and family tragedy, it represented a further diminution of strength for the band's dwindling numbers.

A week or so later, "Sgt. Stewart Albert and a detachment of Company D did see evidence of another massacre about forty-five miles from Fort Craig, where they found a burned wagon, a dead horse, burned articles (including pieces of women's clothing) and a bloody gray hat with a bullet hole near the crown. … He reasoned that the massacred family came from Monica in the San Mateo Mountains, because recent white inhabitants of that place apparently had left in a great hurry. There he saw many signs of both mounted and dismounted Indians."[18]

By the time this incident was reported, Nana and his people were deep in the Sierra Madre. The foray was less a raid than a reconnaissance to allow Nana to survey the current state of white penetration of the Chihenne homeland. What he saw must have depressed and angered him. New Mexico was becoming "The New Eldorado," the *Albuquerque Journal* boasted. "The reports from our mining districts are so encouraging as to lead thousands of prospectors into the mountains from North, South, East and West. New towns are springing up almost every month, new mills are being erected on improved plans, and in every direction we can only see enterprise and development for the better."[19]

---

[18] Billington, p. 102
[19] *Albuquerque Journal*, Dec. 8, 1880.

Tracking Nana

Since Nana and his people had been driven into exile their beloved mountains were filling up with miners and prospectors. Loggers were clear-cutting the virgin stands of ponderosa pine for railroad ties, shoring timbers for the mines and rough lumber for the raw new towns. Texas drovers were moving huge herds of longhorns up into the grassy highlands, competing with Hispanic shepherds bringing their flocks in from the Rio Grande Valley. In all that bustle and activity, there was no place for the Apache.

3

Across the Rio Bravo

"For the Chiricahua, as for all Apaches,
revenge was not primarily a matter of
personal spite. It was a means of redressing
an imbalance in the state of things." [20]

Sometime toward the end of June 1881, deep in the Sierra Madre, the Chihenne held a war dance. One by one the men rose to join the circle stamping around the fire, firing their guns in the air, boasting of the deeds they would perform, and calling out by name the warriors who had not yet joined the dancers. As with most Indian tribes, an Apache's true name held powerful medicine; called by that name he was honor-bound to respond.

Sweeney lists Mangas (son of Mangas Coloradas), Bacutla, Jatu, Sánchez and Suldeen; Kaytennae was another who joined the dance.[21] Lozen's name is not mentioned, although she had returned from the Mescalero Reservation by then. It's hard to believe she would not have been remembered and noted if she was among the raiders, and equally hard to believe she would not have been in the

---

[20] Roberts, David. <u>Once They Moved Like the Wind: Cochise,</u>
<u>Geronimo and the Apache Wars,</u> p. 193.
[21] Sweeney, p. 173.

forefront of a war party setting out to avenge her brother's death.[22]

Nana's reconnaissance in January showed him that the border west of El Paso was too closely patrolled to be crossed without immediate pursuit. Instead, he would move east from the Sierra Madre before striking north across the unpopulated Diablo Plateau of West Texas and on up the spine of the Guadalupe and Sacramento Mountains to the Mescalero Reservation in south-central New Mexico, where he was confident of recruits. From there he would ride west across the *Jornada del Muerto* and cross the Rio Grande back into his home country in the San Mateos and the Black Range. Whatever else motivated him on this raid, the old man wanted to go home to Ojo Caliente.

And all along the way he would leave a trail of blood. In coming months, some Hispanics and at least one Anglo who had proven themselves true friends of the Apache were spared. But many more – including the inoffensive, unarmed shepherds Victorio himself had left in peace to tend their flocks – were slaughtered without mercy.

---

[22] *Both Hutton (The Apache Wars) and Aleshire (Warrior Woman) assert that Lozen accompanied Nana on the Raid. But her Power of sensing the approach of enemies was certainly as important in guarding the women and children as in guiding the raiders, especially since Nana was taking virtually all the band's surviving warriors with him.*

It began June 28, 1881, when Nana and a handful of followers (no more than 15 men and boys) rode down out of the Sierra Madre to attack the Upton surveying party 40 miles south of El Paso, in Chihuahua, Mexico. The Apaches killed four of the surveyors and a teamster. Later the same day and 20 miles closer to El Paso, the war party jumped a stagecoach on the road to Chihuahua City, killing the driver and capturing one unfortunate passenger alive. I've found nothing further in the chronicles regarding the fate of that captive. The next day the Indians "shot up a freight train" on the same road, killing three and wounding several others.

The Indians then cautiously scouted the river crossings below El Paso, probing for a hole in the cavalry screen along the border. Two railroad workers were reported killed about July 8 at a waterhole between Fort Quitman and Eagle Springs, Texas,[23] perhaps by Nana's scouts. On July 13, the raiders crossed into Texas someplace southeast of Fort Quitman, probably close to what was then called *Ojo Caliente* (Indian Hot Springs today).

In 1881, West Texas was a lawless and dangerous country. Mexican bandits, American outlaws, bands of hostile Indians and renegades of all description crossed the Rio Grande in both directions, murdering unwary

[23] Sheridan, Philip H. <u>Record of Engagements with Hostile Indians within the Military Division of the Missouri,</u> p. 116.

travelers and stealing what little portable wealth (mainly horses and cattle) the desolate and unpopulated border country offered.

Defense of the line from El Paso southeast to the Big Bend was entrusted to Col. Benjamin Grierson and his 10th Cavalry, riding out of Fort Davis, Texas. A Civil War hero (John Ford's epic *"The Horse Soldiers"* was very loosely based on his exploits) Grierson was an energetic cavalryman who led from the saddle. Through years of arduous patrolling, he and his men had made themselves familiar with every river crossing and waterhole in their area of operations.

It was this knowledge of the terrain that enabled Grierson to thwart Victorio's attempts to cross the border the previous year, ambushing that canny warrior at Rattlesnake Springs and forcing him back across the river, thus setting the stage for his final defeat by the Mexicans at Tres Castillos.

Perhaps because he was unencumbered by the women and children that Victorio had carried with him, Nana's smaller force was more elusive. He forded the Rio Grande, climbed up Quitman Pass and traversed the desolate Diablo Plateau without being discovered.

In the summer of 1881, Colonel (referred to as "General" by his contemporaries, a courtesy reference to his brevet Civil War rank) Edward Hatch was the much-harassed and frequently frustrated commander of the 9th Cavalry

Regiment and the military district of New Mexico. By an ironic coincidence, on the same day Nana and his raiders crossed the Rio Grande into Texas Sheriff Pat Garrett put a bullet into Billy the Kid at Fort Sumner, finally removing what had been a burr under the colonel's saddle for more than three years. Now Hatch was faced with an even more implacable and dangerous opponent.

That summer the colonel's attention was focused not on the border but on the Mescalero Apache Reservation in south-central New Mexico. Harassed by white stock thieves and "mercilessly and systematically" cheated by the civilian contractors supplying their rations,[24] the Mescalero had supplied Victorio with recruits in 1879-'80, and in the spring of 1880 Hatch and Grierson collaborated in an ill-conceived attempt to disarm and dismount the entire band. That clumsy operation resulted in 30-50 braves fleeing the reservation.[25]

To flush these incorrigibles out of the mountains, Hatch sent to Fort Cummings for a company of Apache Scouts. Nearly 10 years previously, Gen. George Crook had demonstrated to the satisfaction of all but the most hidebound Army officers that only an Apache could catch an Apache. Although Hispanic, Navajo, Papago and Pueblo scouts had all been used in the past, Crook was astute

---

[24] Leckie, William H. The Buffalo Soldiers, p. 194.
[25] Thrapp, Conquest of Apacheria, p. 198.

enough to recognize that even though they shared the same language and culture, there was little feeling of tribal solidarity among the different Apache bands, especially between the western White Mountain and the Chiricahua and Mescalero to the east.

Scouts signed on for six months and received pay and rations equivalent to Army ranks (with tobacco often substituted for the salt pork the Apache detested). Each scout was issued the Army's standard "Trapdoor" Springfield– either the 9 ½ lb. infantry rifle or the shorter and lighter but less accurate cavalry carbine – together with a cartridge belt and Army blouse.

For an Apache male, whose whole identity was wrapped up in his role as a warrior, the gun was a powerful incentive to enlistment, together with the opportunity to once again roam free in the mountains. The extra food their families received was another important spur to men sitting in impotent idleness on the reservation, sullenly watching their wives and children slowly starve on the Indian Bureau's inadequate rations.

Beyond these factors, I believe more than a few scouts joined because they had concluded that the white men were simply too numerous and well-armed to resist, and that the hostiles stood in the way of reaching any final resolution of the conflict that would allow the Apache to survive as a people. Random murders and robberies terrorized and infuriated the settlers but did nothing to alter the strategic balance and only served to further inflame public sentiment on the frontier, where white people tended to blame the reservation Indians indiscriminately for outrages committed by *los bravos*.

To cite just one example, in the midst of Nana's raid on August 6, 1881, *Albuquerque Daily Journal* editor Thomas Hughes thundered: "It is a shame and disgrace that the Mescalaro *(sic)* and San Carlos Indian reservations are allowed to exist. They should be wiped out, and the cowardly wretches who claim protection at these agencies should be killed off."

The message Crook hammered home again and again in his talks with the leading men on the reservation was that the white people caught and punished their own "bad men." Crook warned the chiefs that they must do the same or all would suffer for the crimes of the few. As with the conflicting allegiances in the border states during the Civil War, it was a difficult and painful choice to make. Although generally both brave and trustworthy, the scouts' loyalty could on occasion be pressed too far.

In March 1880 the Army recruited 32 scouts from San Carlos for service in the Victorio campaign. Designated Co. B Indian Scouts, the men were re-enlisted for a second six months in September 1880 and yet again for a third tour in March 1881. The unit was mainly composed of Chokonen, close cousins of the

Chihenne, apparently on the theory that they would be best able to find Victorio in the mountains of New Mexico.[26]

Chihuahua, "the boldest and most respected Chiricahua chief of this time" was named company sergeant, and his brother Ulzana (aka Josannie and other variations) was among those in the ranks.[27]

Chihuahua's son Eugene would later say that "at that time being a scout was not a disgrace, for they had not been used against their own people. When they were, those who stayed with the Army were considered traitors. But even when Chihuahua was enlisted it was a doubtful step." [28]

Both Chihuahua and Ulzana would later switch sides, and it's likely they were already feeling some doubts about their allegiance in the summer of 1881.

Although Chihuahua spoke and understood some English as well as Spanish, Frank Bennett was hired as "chief of scouts" to serve as liaison, interpreter and advisor between the Indians and the officer commanding the unit.[29]

Frank P. Bennett was about 30 years old and had first scouted for the Army against the Cheyenne in Kansas and Colorado more than

---

[26] Radbourne, Allan. *"Dutchy: Indian Scout and Apache Raider,"* True West, Nov. 1998, pp. 38-45.

[27] Sweeney, p. 170.

[28] Ball, Indeh, p. 47.

[29] Sweeney, p. 161.

10 years previously. He had since chased Apaches in the Victorio War.[30]

Final authority and responsibility for the company rested with 9th Cavalry Second Lt. John F. Guilfoyle, 27, an 1877 graduate of West Point.

The company was initially based at Fort Cummings in southwestern New Mexico and tasked with covering the Mexican border. But in May Col. Hatch ordered Guilfoyle and his men east into the Sacramentos.

After their mass exodus from the hated Fort Sumner gulag, the Mescalero had been rounded up and settled on a new reservation in their traditional homeland. But the chain of mountains running south from Sierra Blanca made a tempting natural corridor that the wilder spirits were in the habit of traveling down to West Texas and across the Rio Grande into Mexico. They were joined and encouraged in this raiding by Lipan Apaches, now displaced from their home ranges and all but homeless, and by renegade Comanches escaped from their reservation in Indian Territory.

As a result there was mutual recrimination between the Indian Bureau, the military commanders in Texas and New Mexico and the Mexican authorities. In 1880 the Army tried to solve the problem by disarming the Mescaleros

---

[30] *There was a Captain Frank T. Bennett in the 9th Cavalry, which has led to some confusion, since a chief of scouts was often called "Captain," as a courtesy title.*

and seizing their horses. In the resulting fray a number of the warriors escaped into the mountains, still armed and mounted and now ferociously angry at what they viewed as the white man's perfidy.

According to Lekson, Guilfoyle and his scouts were sent to the Mescalero Reservation in response to reports of Apaches "creating a disturbance in old Mexico and then crossing the Rio Grande below Fort Quitman."[31] But Sweeney writes that Guilfoyle was in the Sacramentos searching not for raiders from below the border but for the renegade Mescaleros, led by a war chief named Manzanita, who had escaped the reservation roundup the previous year.[32]

According to Wellman, "the troops had only the vaguest information" regarding Nana's movements.[33] That could explain why Guilfoyle felt comfortable sending his pack mules in charge of Chief Packer Felix Burgess and a single companion down from the mountains to pick up fresh vegetables at the village of Tularosa.

This is another point in the narrative where accounts differ. Leckie calls it "the train carrying supplies from Fort Stanton to Co. L."[34]

---

[31] Lekson, Stephen H. Nana's raid: Apache Warfare in Southern New Mexico, 1881, p. 13.

[32] Sweeney, p. 173.

[33] Wellman, Paul I. Death In The Desert, p. 197.

[34] Leckie, p.231.

Billington describes it as a train of supply wagons "loaded with provisions from Fort Stanton" for Co. L.[35] Billington identifies the two men with the train as "black troopers" riding mules, while Leckie identifies only one of them as a trooper. There are problems with those accounts – Company L was not Guilfoyle's company and L was at Fort Stanton, not to the south; it's highly unlikely Guilfoyle would have had wagons in the mountains; he had no soldiers accompanying him at this point, and "Chief Packer" is not a military rank but a civilian job title. (Although soldiers could handle mules when necessary, the Army usually hired civilian contractors to manage the animals.)

All the different accounts agree that on July 17 Nana ambushed the little convoy near the mouth of Alamo Canyon (on the outskirts of present-day Alamogordo). One of the men was wounded and a mule killed, the Apaches capturing the other three. Based on the sketchy details available, it's hard to understand how the two packers escaped with their lives. Billington asserts Nana had already been reinforced by "twenty-five Mescaleros," which with his original followers would have given him a 20-1 advantage. But even if Nana still had only his original 15 warriors, it's doubtful that two men – one of them wounded – could have bucked those odds for long.

---

[35] Billington, p. 103.

Tracking Nana

Walking the ground today it's difficult to envision just where the ambush occurred or how it played out. The stony ground at the mouth of the canyon is flat and sparsely vegetated, offering little cover for the attackers. Apaches were famous for their uncanny skill in blending into the landscape, able to conceal themselves in terrain that would apparently leave a jackrabbit nakedly exposed. Even so, a firefight at the canyon mouth would likely have opened at a range of 300 yards or more – which may explain how the two packers managed to escape the trap with their lives. Possibly they were mounted and immediately galloped off, leaving the ambushers to round up the abandoned mules.

Higher up, as the trail climbs the south side of the canyon, there are more large rocks, ocotillo cactus and yuccas that could have concealed the attackers and given them the opportunity to open fire at almost point-blank range. But if the ambushers missed their first shots, the packers might have quickly found cover among the same rocks or behind a downed mule and returned fire, discouraging the Indians from pressing the attack.

According to the *Albuquerque Journal*:

> "A portion of a band of Apaches, supposed to number some seventy in all, attacked the two men from ambush, and began shooting at them from a distance of not more than forty feet, but strange to say, only one gave the trainmaster a flesh

wound in the thigh, and killed a horse or two. Both of the men lost no time in slipping from their horses on the safest side and returning the fire, by which one of the Indians was killed and a slight panic created."[36]

Whatever the circumstances, leaving survivors was a significant tactical mistake on Nana's part. He must have realized that the presence of an Army pack train meant that soldiers were somewhere in the neighborhood and the cavalry would soon be hot on his trail.

The take from this little hijacking was certainly a disappointment. The mules were valuable both as transport and food (Apache epicures are said to have preferred mule meat to either beef or horse). But from an Army supply train the Indians could reasonably have hoped to capture sugar, coffee, tobacco, perhaps even a clandestine bottle of whisky, and – best of all – ammunition. If all they found on Burgess's mules was a load of garden truck, they must have been bitterly disappointed.

According to Lekson's account, Burgess, who was shot in the hip, "struggled back to the (Mescalero) agency, while the other packer, a man named Smith, went on to Guilfoyle's camp to report."

Rather than immediately taking up the chase, Guilfoyle first picked up 20 troopers

---

[36] *Albuquerque Journal,* July 25, 1881.

from Co. L, 9th Cavalry, to augment his force. A detachment of soldiers was stationed at the Mescalero agency, but they would not have been rationed and equipped for an extended field expedition, and as a D Co. officer Guilfoyle had no authority to order men from another unit to ride out with him. Such orders had to come through the proper chain of command. A telegraph line was strung between the agency and the fort in 1881, but it's likely Guilfoyle left his Apache scouts at the agency and rode on to Fort Stanton to report to the commanding officer in person and request assistance.

In the circumstances, it's a little surprising that Guilfoyle was prepared to give Nana a day's head start while he obtained reinforcements. Even if Nana had already been joined by two dozen Mescaleros at this point, Army officers typically acted aggressively in the face of much higher odds. Perhaps the young lieutenant was already keenly aware that instead of hunting Mescaleros with Chiricahua scouts, he was now chasing Chiricahuas with Chiricahuas – men who almost certainly knew each other personally, were related by blood or marriage, and had very likely been fighting side by side against the white man until very recently. In that case, Guilfoyle might well have felt the need for a score of tough, reliable Buffalo Soldiers at his back when he caught up with the hostiles.

Unlike the white regiments, where frequent desertions and low re-enlistment rates often resulted in a high proportion of green recruits, the 9th Cavalry troopers were typically long-service veterans. Proud regulars with years of experience on the Southwest frontier, they were formidable soldiers. In the coming weeks four 9th Cavalry enlisted men and one of their white officers would earn the Congressional Medal of Honor in the pursuit of Nana's raiders.

In the event, the day's delay in seeking reinforcements made no difference. Now with a force of 32 Apache scouts, 20 soldiers and 8 civilian packers, Guilfoyle turned back south to take up the chase. Given the distances and times, I believe that instead of heading back into the Sacramentos he rode west down Tularosa Creek (today's US70) and then south on the flats bordering the mountains (US54/70), a distance of about 40 miles and a hard day's ride for the heavy cavalry mounts.

Whatever his route, on July 19 Guilfoyle's scouts cut the raiders' trail at the mouth of Dog Canyon, about 8 miles south of Alamo Canyon. The trail led west from there toward the *Arena Blanca* (White Sands), and it was very fresh. From the tracks, Sgt. Chihuahua could have told the lieutenant he was no more than a couple of hours behind the hostiles.

Why was Nana still in the area two days after the Alamo Canyon ambush, knowing that the cavalry would soon be after him? According to Sweeney, the raiders stopped long enough to butcher and eat one of the captured Army mules, but that couldn't have delayed them by a full day. Nana and his men could cover ground when they wanted to. From where the raiders crossed the Rio Grande in Texas on July 13 to Alamo Canyon in New Mexico, where they surprised Burgess and his pack train on July 17, is about 120 miles as the crow flies. On horseback, following northeast along the foothills of the Sierra Diablo and then northwest along the Guadalupes and Sacramentos, the riding distance is closer to 180 or 200 miles, an average of 40 or 50 miles a day.

At anything like that pace, Nana should have been long gone two days after the Alamo Canyon fight, but he wasn't. Either he had a pre-arranged rendezvous planned with the Mescalero dissidents hiding in the Sacramentos or like Guilfoyle he rode north to the reservation after the ambush. Nana had lived there for nearly two years in 1878-'79 and a number of Mescalero warriors had ridden with him and Victorio until the Tres Castillos massacre in 1880. Some of Nana's fellow Chihenne still lived with the Mescalero and he was counting on them and discontented Mescalero braves to join his raiding party.

It's possible Sgt. Chihuahua and his scouts were at the agency at the same time Nana and his raiders were somewhere nearby. Whether they ran into each other personally or simply heard rumors, the scouts would know by then who they were chasing.

Tracking Nana

Nana may have been returning from the agency or lingering at the spring in Dog Canyon waiting for the Mescalero contingent to arrive when a sharp-eyed sentry spotted the dust cloud of the approaching cavalry column in the distance. Either way, his enemies were close on his heels when he led out west toward the White Sands 20 miles away.

Kaytennae (also Kaetenae, Kaedine and other variations) was Nana's trusted *segundo*, as Nana had been Victorio's lieutenant. His name meant something like "fights without arrows," a tribute to his verbal skills in what today would be called "trash-talk" – the exchange of insults, threats and vituperation between opponents that traditionally preceded a fight.

Kaywaykla, his foster son, recounted one incident in which Kaytennae was lying in wait on a ledge above a desert waterhole when a group of Apache scouts approached. (Usually traveling on foot, the scouts could easily outdistance the cavalry they were guiding and so were typically ranging far ahead of the troops.) Enraged at the sight of men he knew, Kaytennnae jumped to his feet and yelled down at the scouts, abusing them as cowards and daring them to come up into the rocks. "Come up here we'll give you metal, more then you want. I have sharp metal for your treacherous hearts! Brave warriors who fight their people deserve reward. We'll give it!"

In the late afternoon heat of July 19, 1881, Kaytennae held the rear guard as Nana's raiders crossed the alkali flats and struck the wagon road from Mesilla to Tularosa where it skirted the White Sands.

There, according to Wellman:

> "Guilfoyle's Indian scouts came suddenly upon 13 Apaches at a small ranch house near the Arena Blanca. They had just finished butchering two Mexican men and a woman. So obsessed were they with the work of slaughter that they might have been taken easily. But the scouts were over-eager. Their first shots were from such long range that they were ineffective. Worse, the raiders had ample warning and skipped up among the high hills where it was impossible for Guilfoyle's men to overtake them."[37]

Lekson sets this bloody scene not at a ranch house but beside an overturned wagon, and identifies the dead men as José Provencia of Mesilla and his stepson Victoriano Albillar of Tularosa. The female victim was a 16-year-old girl who had been traveling with her husband, who was missing and presumably carried off by the raiders. The three bodies the raiders left behind were "horribly mutilated."[38] Victoriano, 30, left his widow with a 9-year-old daughter and a three-week-old baby.[39]

We need to pause here, standing figuratively over the corpse of a murdered teen-age girl, to

---

[37] Wellman, p. 197.
[38] Lekson, p. 15.
[39] *Albuquerque Journal*, July 25, 1881.

mourn her senseless death and meditate for a moment on the cruelty of the Apache wars. This will not be the last dead body we will be forced to confront as we trail Nana across New Mexico. Some of them will be soldiers and others civilian volunteers, men who died with weapons in their hands, having accepted the risks inherent in mortal combat against a dangerous foe. But many more will be ordinary people unlucky enough to have been in the wrong place at the wrong time, random bystanders killed in the 19th Century equivalent of a drive-by shooting.

While it's certainly unfair to judge 19th Century Indian warfare by our own standards today, it's significant that these crimes violated the Apaches' own mores at the time. Traditionally, Apache warriors would not kill women or children, or harm an unarmed man as long as he offered no resistance. The Apache today protest they never took scalps until they learned the art from Mexican and American scalphunters, and only began mutilating enemy corpses in revenge for the murder and subsequent decapitation of their great chief Mangas Coloradas.

The nihilistic ferocity of Nana's raiders expressed their anger and frustration. They were men not just grieving the death of their families and friends but facing the loss of their homeland and their extinction as a people.

Of all the Apache bands the Chihenne were the worst treated by the American government, and what makes their destruction all the more tragic is that it was not due to malevolence or even greed but to simple bureaucratic indifference. Although the mineral wealth of the southwestern New Mexico mountains was important in fueling the conflict, the Chihenne need not have been entirely dispossessed to obtain those riches.[40] Cattlemen and shepherds coveted the rich grass in the valleys and mountain meadows, but even today the Ojo Caliente country is sparsely populated by no more than a handful of ranchers.

What really doomed Nana and his people was the incompetence and indifference of Washington bureaucrats who stubbornly refused to even consider the obvious solution urged on them not just by Victorio and Nana but by the soldiers and civilian officials on the scene. Given a reservation around their sacred spring, in all likelihood the Victorio War would never have happened and the Chihenne today would be as settled a people as their cousins the Mescalero. Instead they were relentlessly harried from their home mountains and driven down into Mexico, where they were all but exterminated.

---

[40] *In the event, the boom lasted little more than a decade. When the price of silver collapsed in the 1890s, Chloride, Winston, Lake Valley and the other mining camps quickly dwindled away into ghost towns and the land around them reverted to wilderness.*

Tracking Nana

So our sympathies today are likely to be entirely with Nana – until we confront those three dead bodies on the road to Mesilla. Yes, Indian women and children were killed and scalps taken by Americans and Mexicans alike. But when all is said and done, it's impossible not to recoil in horror from men who would butcher a defenseless 16-year-old girl, whatever their grievances. And a crime like that invites a terrible retribution, the *nemesis* of the Greeks.

There's an old Mexican *dicho*: "Before you ride out to seek revenge, dig two graves."

4

The Sacred Mountain

*"It is a gift to be bestowed
not only for virtue but for
prayer and courage."*

While Guilfoyle's weary troopers rode up to the gruesome scene and set to work hacking shallow graves in the hard ground, the lieutenant was probably asking Sgt. Chihuahua how it was the scouts had fumbled their chance to catch the murderers. If so, it's doubtful Chihuahua was entirely candid with him. According to Sweeney the scouts actually caught up with Kaytennae, exchanged words – Chihuahua presumably urging surrender while Kaytennae returned defiance – and then let him go on his way.[41] Their "long range" shots were a warning to the hostiles that the pursuing cavalry was coming up as Kaytennae followed Nana and his companions west into the dunes of the White Sands.

While the lieutenant and the white scout Bennett conferred, Sgt. Chihuahua may have been sitting by the fire or standing off by himself near the horse lines, watching the sunset over the jagged peaks of the San Andres and thinking about a sergeant's pay. Twenty-four dollars a month was a lot of money on the

---

[41] Sweeney, Edwin R. <u>From Cochise to Geronimo</u>, p. 173.

reservation, and his family ate Army rations even when he was in the field.

But it could be he hadn't really thought it through when he made his mark on the paper and took the blue soldier coat. Leading the buffalo soldiers after the Mescalero was one thing. You might not be easy about it in your heart, but *Nantan Lupan,* the soldier chief the whites called Crook, talked very strong for it. You could sit under the sparse shade of a *palo verde* tree and watch your women try to scratch corn out of the hard, dry ground at San Carlos. You could try to hunt deer to feed your family, or maybe ride south across the line to steal horses from the Mexicans. Or you could hunt men, for $24 a month.

Chihuahua might have considered that hunting other Chiricahua was something else again, especially when one of them was Nana. That *viejo* was crafty and double-tough, and trailing the old fox into those mountains ahead was going to be *muy peligroso* – very dangerous. As Chihuahua rolled himself into his blanket that night he might have remembered Nana's Power over rattlesnakes and resolved to watch his step carefully the next few days.

Led by Chihuahua, Guilfoyle doggedly trailed Nana through the San Andres for the next six days. Nana had a lifetime's acquaintance with those rugged mountains and knew the terrain like the back of his hand. But it's difficult to understand why he would waste valuable time playing cat and mouse with his pursuers in the San Andres when his real goal was across the Rio Grande. Hatch had almost succeeded in trapping Victorio between three converging columns in those same mountains the previous year, and Nana must have realized that the longer he stayed in the area, the more likely the soldiers would draw a similar net around him.

Once he had broken contact at Arena Blanca there was little risk his pursuers could have caught up with him had he ridden directly west to the Rio Grande. Chihuahua and his scouts might have kept pace with the old man, but the troopers on their heavy cavalry horses would certainly have been left far behind.

Guilfoyle's arrival at Dog Canyon may have thwarted a planned rendezvous with the Mescalero renegades the lieutenant and his scouts had been sent to find in the first place. At some point on the raid Nana was undoubtedly joined by Mescalero warriors, but it's not clear when and where they met up. They may have joined Nana at Dog Canyon, or that appointment may have been prevented by the arrival of Guilfoyle and his men. A prudent guerrilla leader might have set an alternate rally point in the San Andres to guard against just that possibility.

But I believe Nana's ultimate destination in the San Andres was Salinas ("Salt Flats") Peak, the Chihenne sacred mountain.[42] It was there that young men went to seek Power. "Those who seek it go alone, that they may be tested for worthiness," Kaywaykla later told Eve Ball. "It is a gift to be bestowed not only for virtue but for prayer and courage."[43]

On the Sacred Mountain Nana would have been able to renew his Power and commune with the Mountain Spirits, gathering his strength for the next phase of the raid. Meanwhile, the Apaches were discovering that the hated prospectors were penetrating even into these remote mountains. On July 24, the hostiles attacked a mining camp at the northern end of the San Andres, killing one man and stealing two horses and a mule.[44]

After a weary week of searching the rocky, barren mountains, Guilfoyle finally caught up with the hostiles in a canyon at the north end of the San Andres, somewhere near the pass that separates that range from the Oscuras. As always, there is some variation in the details in different accounts. Wellman reports the soldiers surprised Nana's band encamped, captured 14 horses as well as blankets and provisions, and wounded two of the hostiles.[45]

---

[42] *At 8,965' Salinas Peak is the highest point in the San Andres Mountains and is said to offer superb 360° views over much of central New Mexico. Unfortunately the mountain is now on White Sands Missile Range and public access is strictly forbidden.*

[43] Ball, <u>Victorio,</u> p. 11.

[44] Kühn, <u>Chronicles of War</u>, p. 243.

Tracking Nana

According to Thrapp the "soldiers captured a couple of horses, twelve mules, all of Nana's camp supplies, and believed they had killed two hostiles."[46] According to Bennett's account, one of the hostiles was shot by Chihuahua.[47] If so, that should have relieved any doubts the young lieutenant might have been harboring about the reliability of his Apache scouts.

Whatever the actual casualty count, Nana and his band were not badly hurt by this skirmish. A wounded man (if there were any) would either keep up or drop off into the mountains, where he would either heal himself or die alone. "March or die," is the unofficial motto of the French Foreign Legion, but Nana and his men would have recognized and respected that hard truth. There was no room in their world for weak sentiment. As to "camp equipment," the raiders carried little more than a few blankets and perhaps a cooking pot, all of which they could do without. Whether horses or mules, the animals captured by the soldiers were likely broken down by hard travel in the mountains and would have proved a hindrance rather than an asset to the Apaches in their flight.

---

[45] Wellman, Paul I. Death in the Desert, p. 198.

[46] Thrapp, Dan L. The Conquest of Apacheria, p 213.

[47] Thrapp, Thrapp, Dan L., ed. Dateline Fort Bowie; Charles Fletcher Lummis Reports on an Apache War, p. 158.

Guilfoyle must have felt profoundly discouraged as he watched Nana's band melt back up into the mountains. Two prospectors who encountered the lieutenant and his men shortly after the fight found him "hatless, coatless, weary and worn," while scout Bennett "had been thrown by his horse and could hardly sit up."[48]

Chihuahua and his Apache scouts were still combat effective, but tough as they were most of Guilfoyle's black troopers were probably close to the end of their endurance. It's worth remembering that cavalrymen walked as much as they rode, since a prudent commander had his men dismount and lead their horses half the time on an extended march. Even with that routine, the grain-fed cavalry horses were certainly broken down by a week of hard work on the scant graze available. The rations drawn at Fort Stanton must have been almost exhausted, and water, as always, was a constant worry.[49]

Despite all this, Guilfoyle doggedly continued the chase, following the hostiles' trail across the Jornada del Muerto, crossing the new railroad tracks near Round Mountain and through the pass between the Fra Cristobal

---

[48] "Murderous Mescaleros," *Albuquerque Daily Journal*, July 25, 1881.

[49] *The springs in the San Andres were dangerous; a whole company had been laid low by gypsum poisoning during the chase after Victorio the previous year.*

and Caballo Mountains to the banks of the Rio Grande. The war party crossed the river about six miles south of the little village of San José (now drowned beneath the murky waters of Elephant Butte Reservoir). On July 28, near the mouth of Cuchillo Negro arroyo (now near the north end of the town of Truth or Consequences) the hostiles killed two men at the ranch of José and Merced Montoya and another two men at another nearby ranch.[50] According to Lekson, they killed two miners and "at least four Mexican sheepherders" as they climbed into the foothills of the San Mateos.[51]

According to Charles Francis Lummis, the newspaperman who interviewed Scout Bennett five years later, the Apaches also carried with them "three Mexican boys captive."[52] In previous outbreaks the Chihenne had generally spared the isolated Hispanic ranchers and shepherds, who often served as a valuable source of information and sometimes arms and ammunition. But presumably vengeance for Tres Castillos could be visited as appropriately on defenseless New Mexico Hispanics as on Anglos.

The *Journal* reported 11 Mexicans killed at *Paraje* (a "stopping place or campground" now like San Jose lost forever under the waters of

---

[50] Kühn, Chronicles of War, p. 244.
[51] Lekson, Nana's Raid, p. 16.
[52] Thrapp, Dateline Fort Bowie, p.157.

the reservoir). "One Indian was taken prisoner and burned alive at the stake," according to the *Journal,* and the hostiles, led by "young Nana," were reportedly "making for their old reserve near Ojo Caliente."[53]

The contemporary newspaper accounts are no more reliable than today's evening news, however. Other accounts mention no Indian captured and most agree on a figure of eight killed – two ranchers near the river and two prospectors and four shepherds killed as the raiders moved northwest into the mountains.

There are several canyons leading into the San Mateos from the east that would present no obstacle to an Apache. But I believe it likely Nana and his band instead followed the Rio Alamosa west (along what is today NM142) up to the little village then known as *Cañada Alamosa* and today called Monticello. A few miles beyond is the narrow canyon that leads to the sacred warm spring, and Nana was aiming for those healing waters.

But on July 28, after he had received report of the war party crossing the railroad tracks headed for the Rio Grande, Hatch had ordered Co. D across the San Mateos to occupy the abandoned Ojo Caliente agency. Although these troops missed encountering the war party, it could be their presence blocked the Indians from reaching the spring. Warned off, Nana would likely have turned north up Rock

---

[53] *Albuquerque Journal*, Aug. 3, 1881.

Springs Canyon on today's FR139 toward Luna Park.

At this point Guilfoyle had been forced to temporarily abandon the chase and ride north to Fort Craig to re-provision. But by the time the raiders disappeared into the San Mateos, the people in the southern half of New Mexico Territory were thoroughly alarmed, as we would be today if a gang of violent criminals were running loose on a murderous rampage across the countryside. And while some frightened and indignant citizens besieged Santa Fe and Washington with demands for protection, others were taking the field to confront the threat directly.

Army officers were generally strongly opposed to citizen posses, militias and other ad hoc civilian initiatives in the Indian wars. True, a band of civilian volunteers from Hillsboro had saved the buffalo soldiers from disaster in a fight with Victorio in the fall of 1879, but in general the Army had good reason to regard amateur Indian fighters as more hindrance than help. That would certainly prove to be the case in the summer of 1881.

Despite the disapproval of the regulars, the Western frontier was peopled by tough, independent men with a strong vigilante tradition. At the end of July Chloride and Fairview (now Winston), the twin mining camps in the Black Range most directly threatened by Nana's raiders, mounted a posse of three dozen miners, local ranchers and farmers, "all under the leadership of a prominent citizen named James Mitchell" to pursue the hostiles.[54]

According to the *Albuquerque Journal* the posse consisted of nine men from Chloride and Fairview, led by "Constable Frank Mitchell," with another 30 men recruited from Cuchillo Negro, San José and Cañada Alamosa.[55] While these communities traditionally maintained mutually beneficial if not always friendly relations with the Apaches, the murders of Hispanic ranchers and shepherds Nana's men had committed on crossing the Rio Grande presumably motivated them to join in the hunt for the marauders.

Based on the outcome of the expedition it seems unlikely Mitchell or any of his volunteers had previous experience fighting Apaches. Wellman says the posse was following Nana's trail,[56] but according to Thrapp, the posse had found "no trace of the illusive *(sic)* warriors" by the time they stopped for dinner at a spring in Red Canyon the afternoon of Aug. 1.[57]

Given their feckless conduct it's unlikely the men had any apprehension the Indians were anywhere in the neighborhood. I believe Nana was descending the canyon from the other side of the mountains, not coming up from the plain.[58] What horses or mules the raiders still

[54] Lekson, Nana's Raid, p. 19.
[55] *Albuquerque Journal*, Aug. 3, 1881.
[56] Wellman, Paul I. Death In The Desert; p. 199.
[57] Thrapp, Dan L. The Conquest of Apacheria; p. 213.

possessed would have been badly used up by the time they descended into the upper reaches of Red Canyon. The band of horsemen riding so carelessly up the canyon must have seemed a gift from the Twin War Gods.

Nana placed most of his force on the cliffs, with a few of his boldest warriors concealed in the brush along the sides of the canyon. The riders unsaddled and set their horses to graze under the protection of a guard while the rest of the men had dinner and then retired for a siesta under the inviting shade of the cottonwoods. Thus they were literally caught napping when shots rang out from the heights above and a handful of Indians sprang out of the underbrush, waving blankets and shouting to stampede the horse herd down the canyon,

By the time the dust cleared the posse had lost one man killed and seven wounded (one mortally) and all their horses were between the knees of Nana and his warriors. The hapless Indian fighters couldn't even claim their return fire had hit any of the raiders. Defeated, dismounted and discouraged, there was nothing to do but trudge back home on foot, carrying their wounded with them.

---

[58] *There is are two Red Canyons as well as a Red Rock Canyon in the San Mateos; both Lekson and Sweeney place this encounter in East Red Canyon, while Frank Bennett told Lummis it was Red Rock Canyon. I believe the ambush actually occurred in West Red Canyon.*

Tracking Nana

At the mouth of Red Canyon, the posse members may have encountered Lt. Guilfoyle, whose men were burying the remains of yet another victim – a lone *pastor* Nana's men had murdered on their way out of the canyon. The lieutenant's reaction on hearing the posse's sad tale can be imagined. Their amateur carelessness had gifted Nana with three dozen fresh mounts, while Guilfoyle and his troopers were almost certainly still riding the same tired horses they had left Fort Stanton on two weeks and hundreds of hard miles before.

The good news was that Guilfoyle now knew where the raiders were, they had left a broad trail for him to follow, and he was only a few hours behind them.

Guilfoyle could have spent no more than a day at Fort Craig before returning to the pursuit. From Craig he probably rode south and then west and north around the San Mateos, his movements part of Col. Hatch's grand plan for corralling the marauders before they did more damage. Patrols from Forts Craig and Selden were deployed to prevent Nana from re-crossing the Rio Grande and heading back east toward the Mescalero Reservation, while detachments from Forts Cummings and Bayard were to catch the raiders if they tried to turn south to Mexico.

Guilfoyle's swing around the southern and western face of the San Mateos was intended to intercept Nana on the assumption the raiding party would make for the Black Range and from there either head south to Mexico or west to the San Carlos Reservation in Arizona. As commander of the New Mexico Military District, Hatch would probably have been only too happy to see the raiders cross into Arizona Territory, where they would no longer be his problem.

But from Red Canyon Nana headed neither west nor south but north, because the old man had another objective in mind. He rode along the foot of the San Mateos for a few miles, roughly following what is today NM52, and then turned up Bear Trap Canyon, a narrow defile that cuts NNE into the mountains toward Mount Withington.

Along the way, Nana stopped first at Frank Pierce's ranch and captured him, then went on to Joseph Ware's spread farther up the canyon, where the raiders captured that rancher, his brother, and his family – all without a shot fired. The captives were forced to stand outside in the rain (an ordeal in itself, as anyone who has ever been caught in a summer thunderstorm in these mountains can testify) while the Apaches looted the Ware ranch house, but it appears that neither Pierce nor the Wares were otherwise physically harmed.[59]

The raiding party lingered at Ware's for five hours, probably because of the rain. What is now Cibola FR 549 up Bear Trap Canyon is little improved today from what it was more

---

[59] Sweeney, pp. 174-76.

than 130 years ago, and I've known flash floods to completely wipe out sections under a heavy rain. Even if he knew or suspected pursuit was close behind, Nana may have had little choice but to wait for the rain to let up before pushing on up the canyon.

His next stop, about a mile above Ware's ranch, was at a sawmill run by Robert H. Stapleton. I believe this may have been near the site now known as Hughes Mill, a tiny Forest Service campground near the upper reaches of Bear Trap Canyon. Stapleton was a 53-year-old ex-soldier who had formed a friendship with Nana when he was working as a civilian employee at the short-lived Tularosa Agency and later at Ojo Caliente. Whatever kindnesses he had done Nana and his people in the past certainly saved Bob Stapleton's life that day, and probably the lives of his neighbors as well.

Nana spoke no English, but Stapleton had been employed as an interpreter at Tularosa[60] and so must have had some fluency in Apache as well as Spanish. That afternoon was the only occasion on which Nana tried to explain himself to a white man, and so it's worth pausing to consider his remarks.

"We have killed everybody we came across so far, and after we leave here we will kill everybody we meet again," Nana told him. He rejected Stapleton's suggestion that he give up.

---

[60] Thrapp, Victorio, p. 149.

"There's no place for me here anymore. Everywhere I go, they shoot at me. I'm ready to die anytime."[61]

Perhaps it was that same grim fatalism that led him to tell Stapleton what he planned to do next, even though he must have realized that while this white man might be a friend, he was bound to tell the soldiers whatever he learned that could help them catch the raiders. Gesturing at two young Chihenne warriors behind him, Nana told Stapleton, "This is all that I have left of my once powerful band." Now, he said, he was on his way north to Navajo country.

"I want to try and get some Navajos with me," he said before he rode away. "Soldiers, miners, ranchers, everyone is against me, and I must get help or they will get me soon." With that, Nana "borrowed" two mules from Stapleton – presumably to carry the loot from the Pierce and Ware ranches – promising to return them when the two men next met, and rode on up the canyon.

"Come, there are bloodhounds on our trail," he called to his men as he led out. Stapleton never saw the old man again.

Estimates of the number of warriors in Nana's raiding party at any given time vary from as few as a dozen to 70 or more. Higher figures can be discounted as either panicky rumor repeated in the newspapers or by

---

[61] Sweeney, p. 175.

military reports seeking to excuse a defeat. And Apaches generally refused to stand still long enough to be accurately counted. In a firefight in a desert canyon, with heads popping up and down from behind rocks, sudden puffs of gunsmoke, the echoing bang of rifles, the whine of ricocheting bullets and a rain of razor-sharp arrows arcing in from unexpected directions, it was easy for even an experienced soldier to over-rate the opposition.

Nana had 13 followers with him when he exited Red Canyon, according to Sweeney, and in Bear Trap Canyon we have a rare snapshot of the band as it existed that day. Stapleton was an eyewitness and a veteran, not just of some Civil War militia regiment but an experienced regular, honorably discharged from the 2nd Dragoons in 1854. He counted a dozen Indians and said Nana told him he had 10 Mescalero and 2 Navajo riding with him. Stapleton also reported seeing a young Hispanic boy with the raiders; the boy had been captured in the San Mateos, where he was herding sheep with two men who were both killed by the Apaches. Counting Nana, the two young Chihenne warriors and the young boy would make a total of 16 riders.

Ware, another eyewitness who had no motive to misrepresent numbers and was apparently resident in the country long enough to distinguish one Indian from another, reported 20 riders – including seven Chihenne, seven Mescalero, and two Navajo. With Nana and the two Chihenne warriors he pointed out to Stapleton and the Mexican boy that would make a total of 20. The exact number in the raiding party at that point is not as significant as the confirmation that Nana had succeeded in recruiting at least a handful of warriors from the Mescalero Reservation.

But where did the two Navajo braves come from?

And where, in the meantime, was Lt. Guilfoyle, his Apache scouts and his detachment of buffalo soldiers?

Stapleton reported that Nana stopped at his mill between two and three o'clock in the afternoon, and from his account of his conversation with Nana it's clear the ambush in Red Canyon had occurred the previous afternoon. If Guilfoyle arrived at Red Canyon in time to encounter the footsore posse, he might have been no more than a few hours behind Nana at that point. While Nana's progress up Bear Trap Canyon the next day was delayed by the heavy rain, it may be that instead of following the war party up the canyon, Guilfoyle took counsel with Bennett and Chihuahua and devised an alternate plan.

From the upper reaches of Bear Trap Canyon, with a herd of more than three dozen horses and mules, Nana had three choices. He could turn northwest on what is today FR 476 into Point of Rocks Canyon, descending from the mountains onto the Plains of San Augustin, Or he could go south and then east, climbing the shoulder of Mount Withington on what is today FR138, a narrow and precipitous trail that leads to FR330 and ultimately (with luck, a good vehicle and determination) to NM 107. That route would use up his horses and bring him closer to Fort Craig. Or he could continue straight north over Monica Saddle and down Monica Canyon.

It must have been clear to Guilfoyle that a "stern chase" into the mountains was a fool's errand. Nana had relatively fresh horses with remounts for every man, while Guilfoyle's own mounts were nearly used up. Plus, Nana had just shown that he was perfectly ready to turn and snap at the hounds when the opportunity offered. Trailing the Apaches into the steep defiles of Bear Trap Canyon would require a high degree of caution, further slowing the pursuit.

But there was an alternative. Nana had to come out of the mountains somewhere. Like sharks, a raiding party had to keep moving or die. If he lingered too long in the San Mateos the Army would inevitably tighten a noose around him. So Nana had to exit the mountains someplace, and soon. The trick was to guess where that would be and to be waiting there when he showed up.

Picture the San Mateos as the face of a huge clock. At the mouth of Bear Trap Canyon Guilfoyle was at 8 o'clock, Point of Rocks 10 o'clock, Monica Canyon 12 o'clock. Guilfoyle could guess that the rain would slow the hostiles as they rode up Bear Trap Canyon. By riding hard around the shoulder of the mountains, there was a chance he could be waiting at Monica Spring when Nana and his men rode down out of the canyon.

It was a bold plan, and it almost worked.

After a long ride around the mountains, Guifoyle and his men arrived at Monica Canyon the next day. But instead of surprising Nana in an ambush they found the raiders already watering their horses at the spring. Soldiers, scouts and hostiles exchanged fire without any decisive result. As in the San Andres, Guilfoyle claimed to have wounded two of the raiders and captured 11 horses, but Nana and his men disengaged either by retreating back up the canyon or swinging around Guilfoyle's flank and riding out onto the Plains of San Augustin.

For the cavalry, the skirmish at Monica Spring was a small tactical victory at best; Guilfoyle had momentarily thwarted Nana's move north to Navajo country, but the hostiles were not badly hurt in the encounter and they could quickly replace the lost stock at the next ranch they came to. But the hard ride had used up the troopers' horses. Guilfoyle could do no more than detach Bennett and his scouts to stay on Nana's trail, while the lieutenant and his weary soldiers camped at the spring to recuperate.

Bennett and his scouts fought a 16-mile running battle with the hostiles as they escaped from Monica Spring toward the Datil

Mountains,[62] roughly along the route of today's US60. Then as now the Plains were open grassland with scarcely a tree or bush in sight. The terrain is not as flat as it appears from a distance, but a gently rolling landscape. By dropping one or two rear guards with good rifles on a rise, Nana could keep pursuers at a distance.

Bennett would have sent one of his scouts back to pick up the cavalry and guide them back on the trail, and Guilfoyle almost certainly dispatched a courier to the nearest telegraph line with a report updating Col. Hatch on the unexpected direction the hunt was taking. On August 6, three days after the skirmish at Monica Springs, two companies of the 9th Cavalry rode out of Fort Wingate headed south and east in an attempt to head Nana off.

One of these patrols, a 15-man force of Co. K led by Lt. Henry Wright, encountered Guilfoyle "north of Monica Springs" on August 9, six days after the fight there.[63]

Nana probably entered the Datils through Main Canyon, climbed up past Blue Spring and descended the north side of the mountains down Red Canyon. Guided by the two Navajo renegades Stapleton had seen with him at the mill, Nana was on his way to meet friends among the people today known as the Alamo

---

[62] Thrapp, Dan, ed. <u>Dateline Fort Bowie</u>, p.158.
[63] Lekson, <u>Nana's Raid</u>, p. 21.

Band Navajo, somewhere in the rugged country west of Ladrone Peak.

Separated from the Big Rez by the Zuni, Acoma and Laguna pueblos, the history of the Alamo (sometimes referred to as the Puertecito) people is murky. Some say they are descendants of the few survivors crafty and determined enough to evade "Rope Thrower" Carson's 1864 roundup and the subsequent "Long Walk" to Bosque Redondo. But some of the words in their language and some of their names are clearly Apache in origin. It's likely some refugees escaped the closing of the Ojo Caliente Reservation and the forced exile to San Carlos by melding into the little Navajo bands scattered through the rough country west of Sierra Ladrone.

Whatever their origins, in 1881 – more than a decade after the chastened Navajo had been allowed to return to their homeland – there were small groups of these Indians scattered in the mountains and canyons south of the Navajo reservation, and they included men like Nana who were yet unreconciled to defeat.

It was a hard existence on marginal ground. By their own tradition, Apaches had once been agriculturists, until they were driven into the mountains by Spanish slave raids – the Chihenne were growing crops at Ojo Caliente before they were forcibly removed to San Carlos in 1877,[64] and the Navajo were sheep-herding

---

[64] Faulk, Odie B. Crimson Desert. New York, 1974, p. 177.

63

pastoralists, rich in orchards and fields before the Long Walk. But now the best farming and grazing lands were being taken up by Hispanic and Anglo homesteaders, the mountains were full of miners and loggers, and the wild game was hunted almost to extinction. The ecological niche remaining for the few Navajo and Apache holdouts still off the reservations was being squeezed to the vanishing point. They were men who "carry their lives on their fingernails," in the words of another Apache chief in similar circumstances,

In 1877, Victorio brought his followers close to Fort Wingate (near present-day Grants) and indicated their willingness to settle near there. It's indicative of their growing desperation that he and his people were prepared to accept a reservation that was even farther north than Tularosa, which they had disdained a year earlier. The Navajo were agreeable, and the Army was prepared to accept any resolution that would put an end to the long and frustrating pursuits through the mountains.

But the Indian Bureau in far-off Washington was not just indifferent to the Indians' plight but adamant in opposition to their pleas. The Warm Springs Apache were assigned to the San Carlos Reservation; if the Army would round them up and deliver them there, the Bureau would undertake to feed and care for them. But Indians not on their assigned reservation were the Army's problem, not the Bureau's. And allowing any group of aborigines to live where they wanted to live – rather than where the Bureau had determined in its wisdom was best for them – was likely to set a "bad precedent" among the Indian Bureau's other hapless charges.

If that seems bone-headed even by Washington standards, remember that the Indians were not just penniless indigents trespassing on the public lands, they weren't even voters. The Bureau's real constituency was not its official wards but the unscrupulous Western businessmen whose "rings" profited from plundering the pittance Congress appropriated for the upkeep of the dispossessed tribes. And so the Victorio War continued to its tragic conclusion with the near-destruction of the Chihenne people.

Nana was on the Mescalero Reservation when Victorio was negotiating with the soldiers at Fort Wingate, but there was communication between the Mescalero, Chihenne and Navajo. At that time the fugitives were camped in the Mangas Mountains about 90 miles south of Fort Wingate, where they were certainly in contact with the scattered bands of Navajo in the area. Now, with Victorio dead and the surviving Chihenne either penned on the reservation in Arizona or in exile in Mexico, Nana turned to the Navajo for reinforcements.

Whether from the desire for loot, for revenge, or simply from the kinship born of shared grievances, "some ten Navajos, led by Margacito and Cibusto, joined him."[65]

The rendezvous was probably somewhere on Alamocita Creek near the mouth of Red Canyon. With these new recruits Nana may have counted 40 or 50 warriors, but the expanded raiding party quickly split into two or more separate groups and spread out through the region. Kühn lists six separate attacks over the next three days as the raiders struck ranches, sheep camps and travelers from the Datils to beyond Rito Quemado to the west.[66] Altogether thirteen men and a woman were killed and five young boys carried off as captives.

Two graves are still faintly visible today by the side of the road not far west of Red Canyon along Alamocita Creek. The victims were freighting supplies to their sheep ranch near Quemado, according to descendants of local settlers. A third man escaped on foot, "and did not stop running until he got into Colorado."[67]

The two men were reported killed on August 7, although this may have been the date the bodies were discovered and the murders actually occurred a day or two earlier.[68] It may be significant that the Apaches burned the ranchers' wagon in this instance. It's hard to believe that Nana, knowing he was closely

---

[65] Sweeney, From Cochise to Geronimo, p. 176.

[66] Kühn, Chronicles of War, p. 245.

[67] Roland, A.E. "Bob," ed. *"The Ballad of Plácida Romero,"* New Mexico Historical Review, Summer 2011.p. 318.

[68] Thrapp, Dateline Fort Bowie, p. 158.

pursued, would have countenanced an act of destruction that would send up a column of smoke visible for miles – unless he intended it *should* be seen. The Indians were laying an obvious trail to draw the cavalry away to the west.

These decoys probably included both Navajos and Apaches; one incident involved 8 attackers, while 12 were counted in another attack. Somewhere west of the Sawtooth Mountains they scattered, some escaping north to the Navajo Reservation while the others faded into the Mangas Mountains to the south.

When Guilfoyle realized that the tracks he was following were thinning out, there was nothing for it but to retrace his path and try to take up the trail of the main war party again somewhere back on Alamocita Creek. That bitter pill could not have cheered the mood around the campfire, or improved the relationship between Guilfoyle, Bennett and Chihuahua. Guilfoyle and his scouts were back on Nana's track when they encountered Lt. Wright August 9. Tragically, they were by then more than two days behind the old man.

5

Plácida's Sad Song

> *"Farewell unhappy parents*
> *Give me your blessing*
> *And always be careful*
> *In whatever undertakings*
> *With these accursed Indians."*
> *– La Indita de Plácida Romero*[69]

Early on the morning of Monday, August 8, 1881, a band of 19 Indians rode down Cebolla Canyon, which winds around Cebollita Mesa on the border of the Acoma Reservation, east of the Malpais lava beds and today's NM Highway 117 in what is now the Cebolla Wilderness.

So common in its variants as to confuse our narrative for some time to come, it is probably worthwhile to pause here and consider that name. The wild onion (*allium bisceptrum*) is a perennial that thrives in meadows and damp, shady spots at higher elevations in the Mountain West. In New Mexico this common plant is familiarly known as *la cebolla*. Indians and Hispanics sometimes used the leaves as food flavoring, and elk, bear and other wildlife eat the bulbs, although people generally find the taste too bitter to be a welcome addition to their diet.

---

[69] Roland, p. 308.

Tracking Nana

For whatever reason, "cebolla" and "cebollita" (little onion) are common place names in western New Mexico, frequently misspelled by Anglo and Hispanic alike.

In 1881, Cebolla Canyon was a broad, grassy meadow through which a small stream flowed and pooled. Overgrazing, the curse of the West, has since denuded the powdery soil and slashed a deep ravine that now runs in an ugly gash down the center of the canyon. The BLM has dumped tons of rock into the arroyo in an attempt to stem further erosion, but the damage has been done and the canyon will never again be stirrup-high in grass, at least not in our lifetimes.

But in 1881 it was virgin country, rich in graze and water. On a little knoll overlooking Cebolla Spring was *Rancho Cebolla*, home of Domingo Gallegos and his 29-year-old wife Plácida. That morning five of their six children were 40 miles away in the village of Cubero and only the youngest, 9-month-old Trinidad, was with her mother. By the corral below the ranch house Domingo's *compañero* José Maria Vargas was loading a wagon for a trip to Cubero for the annual *Fiesta de San Lorenzo* on August 10.

Plácida recognized some of the approaching riders as Navajo her husband had traded with in the past. Like many other Hispanic ranchers, Domingo probably assumed that relationship conveyed a certain degree of immunity from attack. It's hard to explain his actions that morning otherwise. Whether or not news of the Apache depredations to the south had reached his remote ranch, Domingo should have been put on his guard when he saw that the band included seven Apaches who were strangers to him, including an old man who appeared to be their leader.

Plácida and Domingo were just sitting down to breakfast and it could be they offered something to their visitors, perhaps coffee if there was any to be had. After breakfast, one of the Navajo told Domingo they had been boasting to their Apache friends of his marksmanship, and they were all eager to see a demonstration of his skill. Would he shoot at a target for them?

It's hard to understand why Domingo agreed to that proposal. He was 41 years old and had spent his life on the borderlands where Navajo and Hispanic had been locked in a bitter feud for generations before Gen. Carleton and Kit Carson finally imposed a scorched-earth peace. So he knew something of his indigenous neighbors. Perhaps he saw the challenge as a test of *machismo,* proving to his visitors that he was unafraid and that he trusted them. It could be he relied on the knowledge that, as with most traditional cultures, Hispanic and Apache shared the belief that offering and accepting hospitality imposes solemn mutual obligations on host and guest alike.

Whatever his reasons, he agreed to shoot at a target set up on a nearby fence post. When he had emptied his gun, the Indians shot him in the back. When that failed to kill him, one of them crushed his skull with a branding iron as he lay on the ground. When José Maria came running up from the corral the Indians shot him too. Domingo may still have been alive when they picked him up and threw him into the henhouse, presumably so the chickens could peck at his corpse; José Maria they left lying on the path up to the house. Then the raiders ransacked the house, pulled Plácida and her baby daughter onto a spare horse and rode on.[70]

This sad tale is included here in gruesome detail first because Plácida left us a rare first-hand account of a tragedy that was all too common on the Southwest frontier and has since been dramatized in dozens of Western movies and novels (best told in Alan LeMay's *The Searchers*), and second because it forces us to curb any tendency to romanticize Nana and his men as heroic freedom fighters.

To understand the tragic fate of the Chiricahua, we must confront the reality of the outrages that so inflamed public sentiment against them. Whatever the Indians' grievances and provocations, it's hard to view the treacherous death of Domingo Gallegos and the

---

[70] *Word of Domingo's gun and ammunition are probably what drew the raiders to this particular ranch. Nobody remembers the make today, but it may have been one of the Winchester repeaters the Apaches coveted. Good firearms were expensive and rare among Hispanic sheep ranchers in those years.*

kidnapping of his wife and child as anything but murderous banditry. This and similar crimes explain why the people of the Southwest were clamoring not just for the exile of Nana's people but their extermination, and even 30 years later the governor of Arizona would vow to blow up the railroad tracks rather than allow the Chiricahua to return.

> "Without pausing, except to gather up horses wherever possible, he traversed the desert to La Savoya. There, on August 11th, eight days after the brush at Monica Springs, Guilfoyle, still following, came upon the grim signs of Nana's recent presence to which he was by now becoming so accustomed – two Mexicans, their bodies bearing the unmistakable and horrible mutilations of Apache hatred. The troops learned later that two women had been carried off from this same place."[71]

> "At Las Savoya, N.M. on August 11th, Lieutenant Guilfoyle found that two Mexicans had been killed and two women carried off by the hostiles. " – *Col. George F. Hamilton*[72]

The only *Savoya* listed in <u>Place Names of New Mexico</u> is far to the west of Cebolla Canyon, on the outskirts of Ramah.[73] Does

---

[71] Wellman, p. 201.

[72] Schubert, <u>Voices of the Buffalo Soldier</u>, p.97.

[73] Julyan, <u>Place Names of New Mexico</u>, p. 328.

Tracking Nana

Savoya=Cebolla? In the last quarter of the 19th Century, many Hispanics in rural New Mexico spoke little or no English, while most Anglos had only a rudimentary ear for the pronunciation of unfamiliar words, and their spelling was crudely phonetic. It is probable these different accounts both refer to the raid on *Rancho Cebolla*.

Guilfoyle and Wright arrived at the ranch the evening of August 11, three days after the murders, and found a burial party already at work. Roland (on whose years of invaluable research most of this account is based) believes they were a search party dispatched from Cubero to discover why Plácida and Domingo had failed to arrive for the previous day's fiesta.

An imperfect translation from the voluble Spanish of the anxious and grieving civilians on the scene may have left the soldiers with the mistaken impression that two women had been stolen rather than a woman and her baby daughter. Lt. Wright sent a courier riding north to the telegraph at McCarty's with a dispatch for the commander at Fort Wingate:

> "Lieut. Guilfoil (*sic*) and myself arrived here to-night. Found two men dead and women carried off. Captain Parker is at Alamosa. Lieut. Thomas had two fights lately and captured some stock. Have traveled day and night, and men and stock very much fatigued. Hostiles are between us and the Datil mountains. Suggest to Adjutant General to send troops to Monica and Suera

> to head them off…. Lieut Guilfoil has 25
> men, I have fifteen.""[74]

I have found no other mention of Lt. Thomas or his "two fights lately" in various accounts of the raid. Monica, of course, was where Guilfoyle had last encountered Nana more than a week before at the northern end of the San Mateos. "Suera" is an erroneous transcription of Lt. Wright's hasty 19th Century penmanship, in which "L" looks very much like "S." The lieutenant was pointing to Luera Spring, a favorite Apache campground southwest of Monica Spring.[75]

At this point, "Guilfoyle, his equipment worn out and his men as well, was forced to withdraw for refitting."[76] Lt. Wright abandoned the chase at the same time. In an interview with the *Albuquerque Journal* on August 28, Guilfoil (the Journal's consistent misspelling of his name) said he "followed the trail as far as Savolla, on a line running parallel with the A&P road, from where the track was washed out by the heavy rains and could not be traced. He turned south again from here, but getting no more news of them, and the time for which his

---

[74] *Albuquerque Daily Journal*, August 12, 1881.
[75] *It's less clear how Wright calculated Guilfoyle's force at 25. Guilfoyle left Fort Stanton with 32 Apache scouts, 20 soldiers and 8 civilian packers. Had some of these been left behind at Fort Craig or elsewhere on the trail?*
[76] Thrapp, Victorio, p. 214

scouts were engaged having expired, he run into Fort Wingate."

It's impossible to fault Guilfoyle for that decision. Over the past three weeks, he and his men had ridden and walked from present-day Alamogordo to the vicinity of Grants, a distance of more than 300 miles by today's highways and three to four times as far on the route Nana led his pursuers, over some of the roughest country in New Mexico, much of it still roadless and all but inaccessible today. (Bennett later said he and his scouts traveled 1,247 miles in 41 days.)[77] Along the way they were broiled by the summer sun, soaked by sudden thunderstorms, choked by dust and tormented by flies, living on moldy rations and bad water. Whatever replacement mounts they had managed to scrounge at Fort Craig were certainly as jaded as the horses they had ridden out of Fort Stanton, their uniforms were in rags and their boots shredded by rocks and cactus.

Finally, if he had not lost the trail altogether it had grown very cold. If Nana left Rancho Cebolla on the morning of August 8 and Guilfoyle and Wright arrived there the evening of the 11th, the hostiles were four days ahead of him. Much as he might have wanted to rescue Plácida and her daughter, it was time to quit.

Guilfoyle's long march across New Mexico was an epic of stubborn perseverance and a

---

[77] Thrapp, <u>Dateline Fort Bowie</u>, p. 158.

credit to him and the men he led. But consciousness of their heroic effort could not have alleviated the bitterness the troopers must have felt at finally accepting that they had been outfoxed and outrun by an arthritic old man with a limp.

> "The Warm Springs and Chiricahua Apaches possessed these advantages: They knew the terrain and how to scrape sustenance from it. That familiarity with valley, arroyo, cave and crag had bred in the denizens of the Sonoran desert a physical stamina that allowed them to out distance, out climb, and out scatter any U.S. Army pursuit. It imprinted upon their minds a map of every water hole and yielded up an instant inventory of the best ambush positions. This inhospitable desert, a country so harsh that it could not be traversed, according to one U.S. officer, without the aid of profanity, taught the longtime residents caution, resourcefulness and patience, the requirements for survival in a forge-hot environment in which little survived."[78]

In November, Guilfoyle received a brevet promotion to First Lieutenant "for gallant services in action against Indians at White Sands, N.M., July 19, 1881; in the San Andreas Mountains, N.M., July 25, 1881; and at Monica Springs, N.M., Aug. 3, 1881."

---

[78]HUACHUCA ILLUSTRATED A Magazine Of The Fort Huachuca Museum.

Tracking Nana

Ten years later, after serving as regimental adjutant during the Sioux Ghost Dance unrest in the Dakotas, he advanced to captain. In 1892 he was commander of a troop involved in the Johnson County War in Wyoming, and after a tour overseas chasing "insurgents" in the Philippines he made major in 1901. He rose another grade to lieutenant colonel five years later and to full bird colonel in command of the 9th Cavalry in 1911.

From 1912 until October 1915 Col. Guilfoyle and his regiment were once again defending the border, this time against the turmoil stirred up by the Mexican Revolution. At the end of 1915 he transferred to command of the 4th Cavalry in Hawaii and so just missed the chance to take the field against Pancho Villa the next year. He retired in February 1917 – missing World War I by little more than a month – and died in New Haven, Connecticut, in 1921, age 68. Altogether his military career spanned more than 40 years. Other than his brief interview with the *Albuquerque Journal*, I don't know that Guilfoyle ever publicly commented on his pursuit of Nana or what he may have said or written in later years recalling his experiences.

Frank Bennett returned to Arizona, where he continued to lead Apache scouts, first under General Crook and then Gen. Nelson Miles. With Tom Horn, Archie McIntosh, Al Sieber and a handful of others, Bennett was a member of an extraordinary fraternity, the Green Berets of their day, men who were not only physically tough and courageous but able to reach across the linguistic and cultural gap that separated them from the men they led.

Few came to a good end. Horn became a hired assassin and was hanged in Wyoming for the murder from ambush of a teen-aged boy; McIntosh was dismissed from government service for drunkenness and peculation; Sieber ended his career crippled and embittered, vindictively seeking revenge on the young Apache he blamed for his pain.

Bennett's service earned him a sinecure as a postal inspector in Washington, D.C., but he apparently couldn't remain silent at the perfidious treatment of the Chiricahua by Gen. Nelson Miles, who sent loyal scouts and their families to exile in Florida together with the surrendered hostiles. When Bennett added his voice to Crook's in protesting this breach of faith, Miles – a man never tolerant of criticism, least of all when it touched on his professional and personal honor – may have gotten him fired from the Post Office. He found work as an Army teamster in the Spanish-American War, but reached the end of his rope in Hawaii in 1900 in a scandal lurid enough to reach the pages of the *San Francisco Call* and other West Coast papers.

"Noted Scout Commits Suicide at Honolulu," read the headline of a report alleging Bennet had killed himself after poisoning a woman he had "deceived" and borrowed money from. "I never thought to go this way, but a woman is the cause of it all," Bennett wrote in a suicide note to his commanding officer. "Have faced death for the Government often and honorably, and expected to die facing an enemy of the country I loved. I don't know where I am going, but think it is the hardest trail I ever started on."

Still less do I have any insight into the mind of Sgt. Chihuahua. Certainly nothing he had seen on the long chase from Dog Canyon to Rancho Cebolla would have shocked or even surprised him. But the scouts returned from Fort Wingate to their home station at Fort Cummings by rail, a memorable if not terrifying experience for them. On that long trip on the new railroad Chihuahua would have seen for himself how numerous and active the white people were, busy like ants over the land and as numerous. A prudent man might have recognized that he could no more oppose that frenetic energy than he could stand in an arroyo and stem a flash flood after a summer rain. The only hope for his people was to find some accommodation that would allow them to survive the deluge that was upon them.

But then there was Nana, the indomitable old man who defied the whites and challenged their power and yet remained alive and at large, living as the Apache always had. Thirty years later, Emiliano Zapata – who was in many ways more Indian than Mexican – would say, "It is better for a man to die on his feet than live on his knees." In the language of the Tuareg, a nomadic people of the North African desert, the same verb means "he is free" and "he pillages."[79] Half a world away the Chiricahua would have understood and approved that sentiment.

Guilfoyle discharged Sgt. Chihuahua and the men of Co. B Apache Scouts at San Carlos on Sept. 6, 1881. A little more than three weeks later, Chihuahua followed Geronimo in a mass escape from the reservation. When he finally caught up with Nana in the Sierra Madre sometime later that autumn the two met not as adversaries but as fellow outlaws. Chihuahua would surrender and even don the soldier coat again, only to finally discard it in a dramatic confrontation with the officer who sternly told him, "You can't quit! You're enlisted in the Army."

"I am quit," Chihuahua said, dropping his rifle and cartridge belt at the officer's feet and walking out.

But all that was still in the future. From Cebolla Canyon, our own trail leads east and a few days backward in time, to Rancho Garcia. Garcia, or at least "S. Garcia," still appears on some maps, just off NM 6 south of I-40. But as a place on the ground it's gone even from local memory.

Although in some accounts it's referred to as "Rancho Garcia," this was never a single property on the Mexican model, with a *hacienda patrón* ruling in feudal splendor over

---

[79] Porch, Douglas. Conquest of the Sahara, p. 65.

his *vaqueros* and *pastores* and their dependents. Instead, a "cluster of families" sharing the same surname settled *"Los Garcias."*[80] The construction of the Atlantic & Pacific railroad tracks in the winter of 1880-'81 divided the little community into North Garcia and South Garcia, and presumably injected an exciting but brief bustle of activity before the workers moved on.

The Garcias apparently were uncommonly rich in horses. (It could be a railroad siding and loading pens there made it a convenient shipping point for animals gathered from area ranches.) This circumstance attracted the attention of predators. According to Lekson, Nana and his men appeared at Garcia on August 9, killed six people, and made off with 117 horses.[81]

The raiders also kidnapped a nine-year-old boy named Procópio García, by coincidence Plácida's nephew and destined to be his aunt's comfort and companion in adversity in coming weeks.

Kühn's extensive compilation of sources questions whether this incident actually occurred. Citing several affidavits filed in support of claims for Indian depredations, Kühn lists three Mexicans killed by 15 Chihenne led by Nana on Aug. 10 two miles from Ojo Salado, and 19 horses and two mules

---

[80] Julyan, p. 144.
[81] Lekson, p. 22.

stolen the same day by that same band at Jose Elauterio Garcia's ranch at Ojo Salado. Reports of an attack on the settlement of Garcia are "probably a blurred version" of those incidents, according to Kühn.[82]

Two days later, "two more men were killed and a woman was carried off from the small Mexican town of Seboyeta (also called La Seboya, or La Cebolla), even farther north," according to Lekson.

According to Bennett, after killing six men and a woman at Garcia the raiders "whipped to the east, killing two men and a woman at Servilleta *(sic)*."[83] These accounts are so similar to the attack on Rancho Cebolla and the names so similar (Seboyeta, Servilleta and Sevilleta are yet more variants of "Cebolleta") that, like the confusion surrounding "La Savoya," it's tempting to dismiss these reports as garbled versions of that earlier event, even though Plácida's ranch was south and west of Garcia, not north or east, and her kidnapping occurred August 8 (although Guilfoyle and Wright did not arrive on the scene until Aug. 11).

There is another small town, now called Seboyeta but then known as Cebolletta, to the north of Garcia and another named Sevilletta

---

[82] Kühn, Chronicles of War, pp. 245-46. *Kühn also asserts that Procópio Garcia was Plácida's foster son and was kidnapped along with her and her baby in the raid on Rancho Cebolla, which Kühn dates as Aug. 9.*

[83] Thrapp, Dateline Fort Bowie, p. 158.

southeast of Garcia on the Rio Grande. But I have found no other contemporary press or military reports of attacks on either of those places.

It's very unlikely raiders now so rich in horseflesh would linger in the area for two days after the attack on Garcia. They must have realized that Garcia's proximity to railroad and telegraph would quickly bring pursuit on their heels, and there was no hope of concealing the trail left by a herd of more than a hundred horses. South from Garcia a broad, level valley leads directly into the heart of the Alamo Navajo country. Why ride north instead through the lands of the Laguna, who were no friends of the Apache, all the way up into the foothills of Mount Taylor to attack one of the best-fortified villages in New Mexico?

On the eastern shoulder of Mount Taylor, one of the Navajos' four sacred mountains, the Cebolleta Land Grant straddled the much-disputed borderland between Navajo and Hispanic, and up until the 1860s the town served both as a base for raiding parties and a marketplace for trade in livestock, captives, guns and *aguardiente*. In 1849 the U.S. Army judged both Seboyeta and nearby Cubero to be "notorious hangouts" for slave traders, gun runners and whisky peddlers.[84] The little settlement was surrounded with a 10-foot stone wall surmounted by two watch towers

---

[84] Julyan, p.329.

(*torreones*) and pierced by just two narrow gates, fortifications so strong that on one occasion they stood off a siege by 500 angry Navajo.[85]

By 1881, more than a decade after the Navajo were tamed by the Long Walk to Bosque Redondo and back, Seboyeta's defenses may have been in decay and the townspeople's vigilance relaxed. But even so, it's highly unlikely Nana or any of his followers had anything to do with such an assault simply because they would then have had to turn back south and recross the railroad tracks, riding straight into the jaws of whatever pursuit was being organized out of Garcia.

Whichever of these accounts is true and in what detail is of little consequence. What's significant is to look at the pattern on a map. Nana's raiders were cutting a swathe of destruction in New Mexico from the Rio Grande west to the Arizona line.

Curiously, this week of terror coincided with the Feast of San Lorenzo, which is still widely celebrated in the small Hispanic communities that had taken root in the western part of the territory. The date is said to be of significance in the Pueblo Revolt of 1680, when the Pueblo Indians under Popé drove the Spanish out of New Mexico. You don't have to believe these dates more than coincidence to suspect Nana

---

[85] Robinson, <u>El Malpais, Mt. Taylor, and the Zuni Mountains,</u> pp 116-19.

was trying to incite a wide-scale uprising among the Navajo, who were already deeply discontented with their agent. Later that summer there were rumors of Navajo visitors on the fringe of the San Carlos and Fort Apache reservations. They were said to be trading blankets for ammunition and talking of fighting in the north.

Nana's Raid was terrorism in its classic definition: employing violence against a civilian population to achieve a political objective. When he stopped in the San Mateos to visit Bob Stapleton, Nana admitted to Stapleton what he had already discovered on his previous visit to Ojo Caliente that winter: the Black Range and Mogollons were filling with miners, ranchers were taking up the springs and streams, and farmers were tilling the bottomlands. There was no place for the Apache there.

But there was no gold or silver in the Datils and Mangas Mountains, there were few white men and only a scattering of tiny Hispanic settlements west and north of the Alamo country. Driving those out might force the government to give the Chiricahua their own homeland as the price of peace, at least close to their mountains and independent of the White Mountain and Mescalero reservations.

According to Roland's detailed reconstruction of the immediate aftermath of the raid on Rancho Cebolla, her captors took Plácida and her little daughter 12 to 15 miles east, to a Navajo camp by the Ojo Salado. There "the Apaches made Placida leave her child with the Navajo families."[86]

To the mother it was an act of heartless cruelty, but to Nana it was a pragmatic and even kindly decision. He was determined for whatever reason to carry the woman with him to Mexico, and he knew her baby was unlikely to survive the trip that lay ahead. Better the little girl be raised a Navajo – not as good as Apache, but certainly preferable to death in the desert.[87]

Perhaps in exchange for the little girl, Nana took along with him Plácida's young nephew Procópio García.

---

[86] Roland, p. 293.

[87] *And despite her mother's determined efforts to reclaim her, little Trinidad did grow up as a Navajo, marry a Navajo man, raise her own family and live to old age on the Reservation.*

6

Hot Pursuit

"And so when man and horse go down
Beneath a saber keen,
Or in a roaring charge of fierce melee
You stop a bullet clean,
And the hostiles come to get your scalp,
Just empty your canteen,
Put your pistol to your head
And go to Fiddler's Green."

Just eight of the 9th Cavalry's 12 troops[88] were engaged in the hunt for Nana's raiders, together with two companies of Indian scouts (Lt. Guilfoyle's Co. B Apache Scouts and Co. A Navajo Scouts). Col. Hatch also had eight companies of the 15th Infantry available, but these foot soldiers were useful primarily for guarding waterholes and escorting stage coaches. At least five hastily-organized bands of civilian volunteers also took the field, but these posses generally proved useless if not positively detrimental to military operations.

The regimental rolls show the eight cavalry companies totaled between 406 and 423 men, but they were short of horses. During July and August of '81, the eight troops had only between 251 and 266 serviceable horses, leaving 155 to 157 troopers afoot.[89]

---

[88] In his report to Pope Hatch mentions Companies A, B, D, H, I, K, and L; the eighth might have been either C or F.

Tracking Nana

Assuming his eight infantry companies were the Army's average of 41 men per company, Hatch thus had about 740 soldiers, two-thirds of them on foot, to search more than 15,000 square miles of some of the roughest country in the Southwest. But the colonel did have two advantages in chasing Nana's band. The Chihenne homeland was covered by Forts Cummings and Bayard to the south, Craig and Selden to the east, and Wingate to the north, and the newly arrived railroads and accompanying telegraph lines enabled the Army to rapidly move troops to any point on that perimeter.

A courier brought the first report of the Rancho Cebolla attack to the telegraph at McCarty's on August 12, but by then Hatch already had fresher news of the raiders. On August 11, under the black heading **"Apache Atrocities,"** the *Journal* printed the latest dispatches:

> "The Apache hostiles this afternoon burned the town of Garcia, 20 miles from El Rita, on the A&P Road, killing 5 or 6 Mexicans...Apaches reported in force about fifteen miles south of Acomoe *(sic)*. Five men reported killed; a number missing. Several ranches destroyed...Last night at 6 o'clock, a Mexican was driven in from Garcia's ranch (where) 50 Apaches

[89] Watt, Robert N., *"Horses Worn to Mere Shadows,"* New Mexico Historical Review, Spring 2011, p.200.

murdered 5 herders and 2 boys...three scouts report the band camped at Salt Springs, 15 miles from El Rita." (*El Rito* was a settlement on the Laguna Reservation south of Mesita and west of Garcia.)

With the war party spotted west of Ladrone Peak, the colonel's challenge was to round them up before they could escape back to the south. Although Wright and Guilfoyle had been forced to abandon the chase at Cebolla Canyon, Laguna Pueblo was dispatching a force of 40 men from the north, while another force of 60 civilian volunteers rode west out of Socorro, led by Territorial Congressional Delegate Tranquilino Luna. From Albuquerque the superintendent of the A&P Railroad sent a crew of workmen armed with newly-purchased Winchesters west to McCarty's to guard the line of the railroad.

Nana's best route out of this tightening cordon lay along the Bear Mountains, a narrow and low but precipitous chain that runs south from the Rio Salado. His chief obstacles along that path were the mining camp of Kelly and the bustling little town of Magdalena immediately below it, astride the gap between the Bear and Magdalena Mountains.

Nana's most immediate threat was Captain Charles Parker, who was patrolling the Rio Salado with 19 men from his Co. K, 9th Cavalry. Parker was ably supported in this mission by two excellent non-coms, First Sgt. Thomas

Shaw and Sgt. George Jordan. Jordan had already proved himself a cool hand the previous year, when he led a handful of troopers in beating off an Apache attack on old Fort Tularosa. Now Shaw was about to show his own courage under fire.

The Salado is soft sand in the dry season and boggy quicksand in the wet, limiting the number of crossings and ensuring that any traffic is bound to leave clear tracks. On August 12, Parker cut the raiders' trail crossing the river. He left his supply mules behind and hurried south in pursuit. The patrol found Nana "just outside Carrizo Canyon,"[90] which Leckie places about 25 miles west of Sabinal, a village on the Rio Grande south of Belen.[91]

Contrary most accounts, I believe it unlikely Nana was "intercepted" or "forced" into this fight. Given the outcome it's more likely that discovering Parker was on his trail, Nana chose his ground, deployed his men, and coolly waited for the soldiers to catch up rather than risk a running fight farther south.

It's hard to understand why an experienced soldier would have led his men into the narrow neck of the canyon south of Carrizozo Spring without first clearing the heights above. Looking at the broad trail left by Nana's horses leading up the canyon, Parker may well have scented trouble. As a captain in the 17th Illinois

[90] Lekson, p.22.
[91] Leckie, p. 232.

Tracking Nana

Cavalry he had chased rebel "bushwhackers" like Bloody Bill Anderson in Missouri in the last years of the Civil War and he had served with the 9th through the Victorio campaign, so he knew something of irregular warfare.

But he was in a hurry. Nana had slipped past him at the Rio Salado and was riding hard for the Magdalenas, and the captain knew he would never catch the hostiles once they reached those rugged mountains. Nana was encumbered by his captives and a herd of loose stock, but that also meant he had fresh remounts available for his men, while Parker's weary troopers were on the same tired horses they had been riding for a week. If he was to catch the old man, Parker needed to push his men and horses – and his luck – to the limit of endurance.

In his after-action report, the captain estimated he was facing 40 guns, which may indicate that Nana had not yet parted company with most of his Navajo and Mescalero allies, or Parker may have been attempting to excuse the outcome of the engagement. And although Leckie makes it sound as though Parker knew he was engaging Nana's full force when he boldly "attacked at once," the hostiles would scarcely have lined up on the heights to be counted while the captain paused to survey the terrain ahead through his field glasses. Instead, they would have lain carefully concealed until the soldiers were well advanced into the trap. Looking up the canyon, the captain may have calculated he might be facing no more than a few stay-behinds Nana had dropped off to delay pursuit. If that was the case, playing a dangerous game of hide and seek to flush a couple of snipers out of the rocks above was a waste of valuable daylight.

Based on the terse wording of the subsequent Medal of Honor citations, it seems the captain may have detached Sgt. Jordan with a few men to scramble up the more gradual slope on the right and lay down a suppressing fire on the opposite cliffs while Parker and Shaw led the rest on a rush through the narrows up to Barrel Spring. That would place them in the rear of any riflemen on the cliffs, and once those were mopped up Parker could regroup and push on after the main body of the war party.

That was a highly risky tactical disposition, however. If the volume of fire was heavier than expected or better aimed, a couple of downed horses or a man shot from the saddle might have disrupted the advance and driven the troopers to ground. While the men might find concealment in the underbrush, horses were notoriously poor at seeking cover and made the largest and most exposed targets. With Parker and Shaw pinned down, some of the hostiles who had been posted on the other side of the crest to the right could slip around to isolate Jordan's flankers and trap the soldiers in the canyon below. Only the desperate courage of the two sergeants, who stood their ground to hold off the advancing Indians, prevented disaster.

All this is speculation. What's incontestable is that Parker was badly defeated. The *Journal* tallied his losses at one man killed, three wounded, and one unaccounted for.[92] Kenner lists Privates Charles Perry and Guy Temple killed and Privates John Shidell, Wash Pennington and Jerry Stone wounded (the last two so severely that neither ever returned to active duty), but makes no mention of any MIA.[93]

Parker was left in command of the field and claimed his men killed four hostiles, but an objective observer would have awarded battle honors to Nana, who discontinued the action only after he had killed nine cavalry horses and inflicted enough casualties to ensure Parker would be forced to abandon the chase.

"My command dismounted within 100 yards of the enemy, and was vigorously engaged for more than two hours – without shelter or protection, until their whole force retreated to their rear southwest," Parker reported in his "official account of the battle," according to Kenner.

Dismounting for action on foot was a complicated evolution in which one trooper

---

[92] *Albuquerque Journal*, August 16, 1881.

[93] Kenner, p. 149. *In his report to Gen. Pope, Col. Hatch gives the casualty count as two dead and four wounded, while Sheridan's tally agrees with the Journal. Lekson identifies Temple as a "civilian farrier."*

collected and held four horses while his three comrades deployed in a skirmish line. It would scarcely have been attempted under fire within 100 yards of the enemy unless it was simply unavoidable, with men and horses already down and an organized withdrawal impossible. Two of the wounded were hit in the side, which may imply flanking fire (from an opponent above aiming at center mass) as they rode into the canyon, while the third man suffered a fractured skull and internal injuries from his horse falling on him, and so was likely mounted at the time. The two fatalities were both head wounds, possibly sustained by men sheltering behind rocks or downed horses once the company was pinned down in the kill zone.

The fact that Parker lost half his 19 horses would seem to indicate that the troopers were mounted when the action opened, unless the Indians had succeeded in sneaking around their flanks to target the horseholders in the rear.

Jordan and Shaw were each awarded the Medal of Honor for the action. According to his citation, Shaw "forced the enemy back after stubbornly holding his ground in an extremely exposed position and prevented the enemy's superior numbers from surrounding his command." Jordan's citation was almost identical: "At Carrizo Canyon, N. Mex., while commanding the right of a detachment of 19 men, on 12 August 1881, he stubbornly held his ground in an extremely exposed position and gallantly forced back a much superior number of the enemy, preventing them from surrounding the command."

Parker and his men limped back to the nearby La Cienega Ranch,[94] half of them carrying their saddles, while Nana resumed his flight south. There are no good routes out of Carrizozo Canyon to the east or south, so it's likely (as Parker reported) Nana crossed over southwest from Barrel Spring into Abbe Spring Canyon and down what is today Cibola NF Road 123 before turning east through the gap between the Bear Mountains and Granite Mountain just north of Magdalena. As they passed through that night the hostiles killed one man and stole a horse from a ranch in the Bear Mountains.[95] By the next morning they were within a few miles of Socorro after a ride of more than 40 miles.

"Horses move long distances at a fast walk or a slow trot, not at a gallop," Kaywaykla later explained. "They can maintain a pace of five or six miles an hour half the night. When ours became exhausted we changed mounts, preferably to ranch horses roped out as we

---

[94]*Citing Parker's initial after-action report from that ranch, Roland concludes the fight actually occurred not in Carrizo Canyon but in Cienega Canyon, which is north of the Rio Salado. A 1982 archeological survey placed the battle at the west end of the Salado Box, another canyon farther down the river, based on the presence of three graves at that site.*
[95] Kühn, <u>Chronicles of War</u>, p. 246.

went. Our tired ones were loose-herded with us, or if we had them long, they followed."[96]

Early August 13 the hostiles struck a three-wagon supply train camped along the Magdalena road and killed Lee L. Van Epps, the owner of the goods, one of his teamsters, William English, and a traveler named John Herman who was camped with them. Further along the road the raiders killed Juan de Dios Baca and his son and that night they struck Werner's ranch, killing him and capturing his wife, according to the August 15 *Journal*. Kühn gives the victim's name as Andres Warner and places his ranch at Cienega de la Magdalena, 15 miles from San Marcial, but makes no mention of his wife.[97]

There is no further mention of the unfortunate Mrs. Werner (or Warner) in the various accounts of the raid, although on August 17 the *Journal* reprinted a dispatch from the *Socorro Sun* that, "A Mexican boy arrived in Poloodera, *(Polvadera, or "Dusty,")* a small Mexican town ten miles north of this city, on Saturday morning, and reported that he had been a prisoner of the Indians six days, that during that time they killed two Americans and ten Mexicans. The Indians had a white woman and two children as prisoners." That woman may have been Mrs. Werner.

---

[96] Ball, <u>In the Days of Victorio</u>. p.73.

[97] Kühn, <u>Chronicles</u>, p. 246.

Tracking Nana

Apache raiders frequently rode at night across open country to escape observation and rested by day high up in the mountain canyons, where they could usually find water, graze their stock and watch their backtrail during the daylight hours.

The war party likely split up somewhere along the Socorro road, with some bolder spirits continuing southeast toward Fort Craig while the rest, with captives, horses and plunder, rode south into the Magdalenas. Apaches were capable of moving in a disciplined mass like a European force, with a vanguard, flanking outriders and a rear guard protecting the main body. But a war party more typically passed through the countryside like a flock of desert quail moving through the underbrush, or – more appropriately – like a pack of hunting wolves.

Kit Carson vented his frustration in pursuit of another such war party: "the rascally Apaches, on breaking up their camps, would divide into parties of two and three and then scatter over the vast expanse of the prairies to meet again at some preconcerted place, where they knew water could be had."[98]

---

[98] Lynn, Alvin R. <u>Kit Carson and the First Battle of Adobe Walls,</u> p.21.

7

Cuchillo Negro

*"When a man was old he could no longer
get about easily; the labors of the hunt and
the warpath were too much for him; he was
pushed aside by the more active and
vigorous ... How much better, therefore, to
struggle and fight, to be brave and
accomplish great things, to receive the
respect and applause of everyone in the
camp, and finally to die gloriously at the
hands of the enemy!"* [99]

Fort Craig was empty save for three lonely
sentries, according to the *Journal,* with the
whole garrison out chasing Indians. The post
could not have been quite that abandoned,
since Col. Hatch had moved his headquarters
down there from Santa Fe in order to be closer
to the action. But he was certainly running low
on available reserves.

The unusually heavy monsoon rains had
washed out railroad tracks, leaving two
companies of the 9th temporarily stranded in
Colorado and out of play. Worse, the telegraph
lines that should have provided Hatch with a
flow of actionable intelligence instead flooded
his headquarters with wild rumors. Every
isolated little way station on the railroad with a
telegraph key was forwarding exaggerated

---

[99] Grinnell, George Bird. The Fighting Cheyennes, p. 11.

reports of Indian outrages and demanding military protection. A rancher in western New Mexico complained he had successfully stood off "200 Navajo" but the Indians had made off with 300 head of cattle (perhaps some enterprising settlers already had their eye on future claims against the government's purse); a farmer rode a lathered horse in to Fort Wingate to report an entire village massacred south of the Zuni reservation, and a party of "60 or 70" Indians was sighted riding northwest through the Mangas Mountains toward the Arizona line.

By the time the colonel received Parker's initial report of the fight at Carrizo Canyon that bad news was already out of date, superseded by dispatches from Socorro of the attacks along the Magdalena road. Standing on the porch of the commanding officer's quarters at Fort Craig, Hatch may have been able to see the smoke from Werner's burning ranch house. That at least was solid intelligence.

The colonel correctly deduced that the war party was moving south toward the San Mateos, and he had been dealing with Apaches long enough to recognize that Nana was almost certainly headed for the Chihenne sacred spring at Ojo Caliente. If he could strike the hostiles there the long and frustrating chase would be over.

Parker's Co. K was retreating toward the Rio Grande and an exhausted Lt. Guilfoyle with L and Lt. Wright with the other half of K had withdrawn to Fort Wingate. Hatch brought Captain Michael Cooney's A Co. up from Fort Selden to Fort Craig by rail and sent it west through the gap between the Magdalenas and the San Mateos, but these troops passed through the area before the hostiles crossed going south.

Lt. Charles Taylor, with detachments of B and H and A Company Indian Scouts,[100] was next brought to Fort Craig by rail and sent west along the same route with orders to skirt the western slope of the San Mateos and make for Ojo Caliente. Other units were either throwing a cordon above the border to the south or guarding the Mescalero reservation to the east.

With all these troops in the field, the colonel had one last arrow in his quiver. Company I was newly arrived at Fort Craig by train, having just completed a long and demanding march from Fort Wingate down the North Star Road to Fort Bayard near Silver City. Although the company mustered 54 men they shared just 23 serviceable horses, so that more than half the troopers must have been left behind at Fort Wingate. Now, looking over men and horses as they arrived at Craig, the colonel decided they were fit for one more mission.

He had some doubts about the company's young commander, however. Second Lt. George Burnett, 23, was a "shavetail" (a derisory

---

[100] *These were Navajo. Co. A Apache Scouts was at Fort Apache in Arizona.*

nickname borrowed from packers who clipped the tails of untrained young mules to make them easily identifiable) fresh out of West Point. He was an eager and energetic officer; but he had been with the regiment less than a year and he had a lot yet to learn about fighting Apaches.

Hatch apparently judged the force needed more mature leadership for the job ahead, and he put First Lt. Gustavus Valois[101] in as company commander before the troop departed Fort Craig.

Born in Prussia and christened Augustus Heinel, Valois adopted his French name when he emigrated to America and enlisted in the Union Army in 1862. He emerged from the Civil War a captain and served another three years as a non-com in the 5th Cavalry before securing a commission in the 9th. Although he had little experience leading troops in the field, he apparently enjoyed the colonel's full confidence. In October of the previous year, Hatch had selected Valois to command the escort accompanying President Rutherford B. Hayes, General Tecumseh Sherman and the Presidential entourage from the Southern Pacific railhead near Shakespeare to the A.T&S.F. at Round Mountain in the *Jornada*. This was no merely ceremonial honor, as their

---

[101] *"Captain" in some accounts, a courtesy reference to his Civil War rank.*

route took the party through some of the most dangerous Apache country in the territory.[102]

Presumably Hatch hoped Burnett and Valois would balance each other out, with the older man's prudent caution curbing the young lieutenant's aggressive enthusiasm while company First Sergeant Moses Williams would provide badly-needed tactical guidance.

The company marched out of Fort Craig on August 13 and by the morning of the 16th the men were watering their horses in the creek near the little village of Cañada Alamosa/Monticello when an excited young boy rode in to report the Apaches had just attacked the nearby Chavez ranch. Whether the company had arrived the previous evening or just that morning, the men were in the middle of tending their tired mounts when the alarm was given, and most were in no shape to move out. Rather than wait until all were ready, Burnett persuaded Valois to allow him to take those he could mount and start out immediately, while the company commander would follow with the balance of the command as soon as they could saddle up. Burnett took about a dozen men, half the force, and rode for the Chavez place. Along the way he was joined

---

[102] *It was unfortunate Nana was still in Mexico when President Hayes and Gen. Sherman passed through, as he certainly would have valued the opportunity to lay his grievances before the Great White Father and the Army's top general in person.*

by a hastily organized civilian posse drawn from the nearby village and local ranches.

They found Chavez, his wife and two children and two shepherds all dead – as far as I know it was the only occasion during the raid when the Apaches deliberately killed children, and likely was done to enrage the pursuers and overcome their caution. In the distance, little more than a mile away on the bench that borders the Rio Alamosa, Burnett could see a group of men "for the most part dressed as Mexicans with blankets over their shoulders and wearing sombreros, which they waved for us to come on." At first the lieutenant mistook the strangers for more civilian volunteers, but he was soon persuaded these were in fact the raiders, taunting the soldiers and daring them to come after them.

Nana deliberately challenged the soldiers to battle that morning. When they attacked the Chavez ranch, the Apaches could hardly have been unaware that the troops were just two miles away. But instead of riding off they attacked the ranch and then halted on the nearby high ground, "deployed mounted and apparently waiting for some one," according to Burnett's later account, until the lieutenant and his little command arrived. The *sombreros* and *serapes* were an attempt to lure the soldiers into pursuit.

If Nana had known the brash young lieutenant personally he could not have devised a better stratagem. Although Burnett counted

40 Indians on the heights – and some of his men claimed to see as many as 60 – he immediately advanced up the slope at a gallop, without waiting for Valois and the remainder of the company to come up. The fact that the Indians opened fire at more than a half-mile indicates they did not intend to engage their enemies in open country but instead wanted to draw their pursuers into the *Sierra Cuchillo Negro*, a low-lying chain that separates the Cañada Alamosa from the Black Range to the west.

When Burnett dismounted some of his men to return fire and sent others under Sgt. Williams to flank the hostiles, the Indians retreated to the next rise and repeated the tactic. Nana's plan was to lure the soldiers and their civilian auxiliaries into terrain where they could be fragmented into separate detachments beyond the support of the other elements of the command, disorganized and demoralized by unexpected flanking fire from different directions, and then destroyed in detail.

It was an extraordinarily risky stratagem for the Indians because between the Cuchillo Negros and the safe haven of the Black Range were the booming mining camps of Chloride and Fairview/Winston. Just a cluster of tents and a few crude log buildings when Nana passed through in January, by mid-summer Chloride boasted eight saloons, three restaurants, two butcher shops and other thriving businesses, and hundreds of miners were busily staking out claims in the surrounding countryside.[103] By engaging the troops in the Cuchillo Negros, Nana risked being caught between the soldiers in front and the miners to his rear.

Burnett's standard tactic of "fire and maneuver" – establishing a base of fire to keep the opposing force pinned in place while deploying a detachment to swing around the enemy's flank – is the basic small unit exercise still taught to the Army's aspiring second lieutenants today. When repeated several times in rugged terrain against an opponent who is simultaneously trying to work around your own flanks, the resulting collision is likely to lead to some ugly surprises.

While scarcely mountains compared to the Black Range or San Mateos, the Cuchillo Negros are steep and deeply cut by arroyos and canyons that funnel horseback travel along limited routes. According to Burnett's later account:

> "I made a wide detour to the left and on approaching the rear of the Indians my attention was called by Sergt. Williams to a dark object probably 150 yards directly in front of me, and he remarked that he believed it to be the head of an Indian peeping over the rocks. We were riding in "column of files." I sprang from my horse and took

---

[103] Sherman, James E. Ghost Towns and Mining Camps of New Mexico, p 43

deliberate aim at point blank range over my horse's saddle for an instant. The object did not move and not willing to risk giving an alarm I was on the point of withdrawing my carbine when I perceived a slight movement and firing instantly I had the satisfaction of feeling that I was responsible for at least one 'good Indian.'

"Immediately the Indians opened up on us from all along the ridge. I at once ordered my men to dismount and take shelter among the rocks, but in the excitement my horse broke and started to the rear riderless on the dead run. Someone started the cry 'They've got the Lieut.' and with this the whole outfit proceeded to follow suit – with the exception of 1st Sergt. Williams and Private Aug. Walley, who remained by me. I called to Sergt. Williams to go after them and bring them back.

"In the meantime myself and Walley under a heavy fire took shelter among the rocks and returned the fire till joined by Sergt. Williams and the rest of the detachment, he having quickly succeeded in rallying them. "[104]

It was by then four o'clock in the afternoon, and Burnett was wondering where his commander was with the rest of the company. He sent a courier pelting back toward the Cañada Alamosa to urge Valois to come up and

---

[104] Lieutenant George R. Burnett, in a letter to Ordnance Sgt. Moses Williams, June 20, 1896:

take a position on the high ground to his right, while Burnett continued to work around the left in an attempt to block the Apaches' escape into the Black Range.

"Finally we succeeded in dislodging the Indians and a number of them mounted started along the base of the mountains to the left toward the Rio Grande," Burnett wrote. "My first impulse was to follow them, when my attention was attracted by heavy firing on our right, and the remark by Sergt. Williams that he 'believed the main fight was there and that our Indians were only a decoy.'"

By recognizing that the hostiles fleeing to the left were decoys, Sgt. Williams averted what might otherwise have been a military disaster smaller in scale but equal in scope to Custer's five years' previously. Young Lt. Burnett deserves equal credit for listening to his experienced sergeant in the heat of battle and abandoning pursuit of what appeared to be a defeated foe. Instead he moved in the opposite direction and arrived on the scene just in time to save Valois from making a classic last stand.

> "On coming over the intervening plateau I saw at a glance that there was not a moment to be lost for the Indians were concentrating from all directions on Valois who in his efforts to reach the hills referred to above, had been anticipated by the Indians who got there first and gave him a very warm reception. They killed or wounded nearly all of his horses and wounded some of his men

and when we came up he was making his way to the rear as well as possible and the Indians were in hot pursuit.

"There was nothing for us to do but charge them, which I did mounted, and drove them back to cover and dismounting held them long enough for Valois to collect his scattered men and get his wounded to the rear. Believing the Indians to be too strong for him, Valois ordered his men to fall back and sent word to me to follow."[105]

As he was complying with that order, "my attention was attracted by one of Valois' men, whom I believed to be dead, calling to me 'Lieutenant please, for God's sake don't leave us, our lives depend on you.' I then discerned that Valois in falling back had left three men – Privates Glasby, Wilson and Burton – behind some prairie dog mounds about two hundred yards from the Indians and midway between their line and mine," Burnett continued.

While Burnett and Williams provided covering fire, Pvt. Walley rode out and picked up the most seriously injured trooper and carried him to the rear, while the other two wounded men crawled back on their own. Burnett then rounded up the horses Valois had abandoned in his hasty retreat before following the rest of the company back to Cañada Alamosa.

---

[105] Ibid

Although Burnett mentions only "three men wounded, ten horses killed, and several wounded," and makes no mention of his own wounds, Gen. Sheridan's 1882 report lists Burnett as twice wounded and two men killed in the engagement.[106] (It could be that two of the wounded men later died.) According to its muster rolls, I Company had 54 men fit for duty in August 1881 but just 23 serviceable horses.[107] If a dozen animals had been killed or wounded, Nana had effectively converted Co. I to infantry.

"The Mexicans suffered some loss but I was unable to learn exactly how much," Burnett added.

An incomplete victory and an expensive one for Nana's small force, if Burnett is correct that "a number of bodies were found the next day concealed among the rocks." While the old man might have taken some satisfaction in having inflicted a painful lesson in irregular warfare tactics on his opponents, he was in fact only partially successful.

With men dead and wounded, half his horses out of action and low on ammunition, Valois had no choice but to retreat to Cañada Alamosa. That was the problem from Nana's point of view, if his primary objective was to reach the sacred spring at Ojo Caliente. He had

---

[106] Sheridan, Record of Engagements, p. 115.
[107] Watt, Robert N. *"Horses Worn to Mere Shadows,"* N.M. Historical Review, p. 200

tried to draw Burnett off to the southeast and concentrated his force on attacking Valois, intending to eliminate him entirely or at least drive him away east back down to the Rio Grande. That plan had been thwarted by the timely arrival of Burnett and his men, which allowed the reunited company to retire back to where they effectively plugged the only canyon leading to Ojo Caliente from the east.

The soldiers didn't need horses or even much ammunition to hold those sheer cliffs. Just a few months previously, Blanco and a few warriors drove an Army supply column out of that narrow canyon; now the moccasin was on the other foot. Balked just short of his goal, Nana had no choice but to circle around to the west, making a dangerous night passage through the miner-infested hills around Chloride Gulch.

The Cuchillo Negro fight was the only occasion during the raid when Nana took the offensive against the troops; in every other engagement he was defending himself against pursuit. I believe Nana deliberately challenged the cavalry in order to draw them away from their position blocking access to the hot springs. He wanted to visit this, the most sacred place in the Chihenne heartland, for one last time. He may even have intended to make his last stand there, at the head of a nearly impregnable canyon. Victorio, they said, had not been killed by the Mexicans but had stabbed himself with his own knife when he ran out of options. With his chief's death, Nana had lost his dearest friend. His last raid through New Mexico must have convinced him that the future could only hold final and complete defeat. What better way for an old warrior to die but with his rifle in his hands, his face to his enemies and his feet planted firmly on his home ground?

According to his Congressional Medal of Honor citation. Burnett "saved the life of a dismounted soldier, who was in imminent danger of being cut off, by alone galloping quickly to his assistance under heavy fire and escorting him to a place of safety, his horse being twice shot in this action."

Burnett never progressed past first lieutenant in the regular Army, although he later served as colonel of the Iowa National Guard. Severely injured when his horse fell on him, he retired due to his disabilities in 1891. He taught at military prep schools, served for several years at a U.S. consulate in Germany and died in Lincoln, Nebraska, in 1908, age about 50.

Born in Carrollton, Louisiana, in 1845, Moses Williams joined the 9th when the regiment was organized in 1866. He learned to read and write and won promotion to sergeant after just two years in the ranks. He was a veteran of 15 years' service when he fought at Cuchillo Negro. His Medal of Honor citation for the Aug. 16, 1881 engagement: "Rallied a detachment, skillfully conducted a running fight of 3 or 4 hours, and by his coolness, bravery, and unflinching devotion to duty in standing by his commanding officer in an exposed position under a heavy fire from a large party of Indians saved the lives of at least 3 of his comrades." He died in 1899, age 53.

Born in Maryland in 1856 and enlisted in 1878, Pvt. "Gus" Walley was Burnett's "striker" or personal servant, a position officially abolished by the Army in the 1870s but continued informally into the 20th Century. Derided by other enlisted men as a "dog robber," the striker cleaned and maintained his officer's uniform and equipment and generally looked after him in garrison and on campaign. In black regiments, officers and their strikers often developed a strong bond that helped bridge an otherwise insurmountable cultural gap. Walley retired as a First Sergeant in 1907 but was recalled to duty in World War I, retiring again in March 1919. He died in 1938 at age 82 and is buried in his hometown. His Medal of Honor citation reads simply: "Bravery in action with hostile Apaches."

North of the village of Cañada Alamosa, (which officially became Monticello sometime in 1881 with the arrival of the town's first postmaster), Alamosa Creek is squeezed into a gorge now called the Monticello Box. This canyon is so narrow that in places the "road" is in fact the creek bed running between vertical cliffs, so that during the rainy season it is frequently entirely impassable. Valois effectively blocked this direct route north as he retreated to his camp, forcing Nana to follow the Cuchillos north toward Wildhorse Canyon, where he could swing back east to Ojo Caliente.

By New Mexico standards the Sierra Cuchillo is a range of steep hills rather than mountains, but for men on horseback there are only a few routes over the crest. Once over the pass Nana faced a new obstacle – the booming mining camps of Fairview (Winston) and Chloride. Since it was already late in the day when they disengaged from Burnett and Valois in the Cuchillo foothills, the war party likely made this passage that night, emerging into Wildhorse Canyon early the next day.

"Lieut. C.W. Taylor, Ninth Cavalry, came up with the hostiles at daylight in the morning of the 16th, in the San Mateo Mountains, soon routing them and driving them out of the mountains during the day," according to Hatch's report.[108] This date is difficult to reconcile to other reports that Co. "I" engaged Nana's war party at Cañada Alamosa on that same afternoon, unless Taylor had encountered a separate group of hostiles.

According to the August 18, 1881, *Albuquerque Journal:*

> "Yesterday afternoon Lieut. Taylor, with a squad of 30 or 40 troops, was trailing a band of Apache Indians,

---

[108] Lincoln, <u>Annual Report of the Secretary of War, 1881</u>, vol. I, p. 127.

when some thirty miles from Fort Craig, they came upon a fresh band of Apaches, about forty in number, direct from Mexico. A sharp skirmish ensued, lasting over two hours, in which five soliders *(sic)* were killed and several wounded. The Indian loss was severe, but exact numbers not known."

Well, as we used to say when I worked there, "If it's in the *Journal*, it must be true." But no other reports of this encounter mention any casualties on either side and I have seen no reports of any other significant incursions across the border that summer. It's probable the band Taylor engaged was in fact Nana's, and the conclusion that these Indians were "direct from Mexico" may simply have been based on the same sombreros and blankets Burnett reported observing.

Taylor probably arrived at Ojo Caliente on the 16th and was alerted by a courier from Valois that the hostiles were headed in his direction, or he may simply have been sweeping the country to the southwest of the old agency when his scouts encountered Nana's vanguard. According to Lekson there were no casualties on either side in this skirmish, although the hostiles killed several of Taylor's horses as they withdrew west into the Black Range.[109] In return, Taylor's men recaptured several stolen

---

[109] Lekson, p. 27.

horses – likely abandoned as too worn out to keep up with the raiders – and "some of the stolen property" – perhaps the Mexican hats and blankets Burnett had reported.

Nana and his men were presumably exhausted from the previous day's fighting and another all-night ride, as well as low on ammunition. It must have been a bitter disappointment for the old warrior, but his only path now ran west toward the headwaters of the Gila. Once he abandoned the idea of reaching Ojo Caliente, his sole objective was to shake Taylor off completely, or at least kill enough horses to slow the soldiers down. In this he was only partially successful. "Taylor lost a few horses killed, but no men. Nana withdrew once more and plunged into the Blacks, Taylor in close, but slowing pursuit."[110]

Col. Hatch came down from Fort Craig to tour the scene of the Cuchillo Negro fight and talk with Burnett and Valois in person.[111] It must have been an uncomfortable interview. Guilfoyle had missed two chances at the hostiles before losing their trail altogether; then Parker had been soundly defeated at Carrizo Canyon. Now Co. "I" had been beaten and driven from the field, and the hostiles had once again disappeared into the mountains.

For Hatch personally it was a serious blow to his professional ambitions. In the shrunken

---

[110] Thrapp, p. 215.
[111] Lekson, p. 28.

post-Civil War Army there were perhaps half a dozen colonels on active service in the field with a serious chance of winning the coveted general's star, and most of them tried their hand against the Apaches at one time or another with varying degrees of success. Compared to Grierson's defeat of Victorio in Texas the previous year and Crook's earlier achievement in corralling the Western Apaches in Arizona, Hatch and his 9th Cavalry had little to boast of in New Mexico.

Cuchillo Negro was yet another in a string of bitter blows the Apaches had inflicted on the regiment Hatch had personally recruited and led for 15 years. "If it weren't for bad luck, we'd 'a had no luck at all," pretty much summarizes the 9th Cavalry's record against first Victorio and now Nana. In every engagement the Apaches had either won outright or tied the score, killing men and horses before slipping away to fight again. It was not the U.S. Cavalry but the Mexicans who finally trapped and killed Victorio, and now Nana was burning ranches, murdering travelers, kidnapping women and children, and literally running rings around the hapless 9th Cav.

"Sensational accounts of burnings, sackings, and massacres filled the newspapers."[112] Southwestern New Mexico was liberally salted with unreconstructed ex-Confederates with a visceral dislike for black men in blue uniforms,

---

[112] Ibid

and the talk in the saloons was full of bitter criticism both of Hatch and his regiment. (In Silver City the previous year a crowd celebrated the glad news of Victorio's death in Mexico by burning Hatch in effigy.) If Nana escaped back across the border now, he was carrying Hatch's hopes of promotion with him.

Hatch sent Valois and his men together with Cooney's troop into the Black Range in pursuit of the hostiles and concentrated the remainder of his forces at the bottom of the sack to block the southern exits from the mountains. Then the colonel boarded a train south to Fort Cummings, where he intended to take personal charge of salvaging his own and his regiment's reputations by capturing or destroying Nana and his band.

8

Ambush in Gavilan Canyon

I seek for one as fair and gay
But find none to remind me
How sweet the hours I passed away
With the girl I left behind me

Sometime during the day of August 18, two days after the Cuchillo Negro fight and one day after Taylor chased Nana into the Black Range west of Ojo Caliente, mounted raiders galloped through the little tent camp of Gold Dust, shooting wildly and yelling in what Texas cowboys on a spree in a Kansas cowtown would have called a "hooraw." The miners were apparently all out in the hills working their claims and the few women and children remaining in camp were terrified but unhurt.[113]

Gold Dust was south of Hillsboro, just a few miles from the raw new mining town of Lake Valley on the southeastern flank of the Mimbres Mountains. That's about 50 miles as the crow flies and more than 120 by road from Wildhorse Canyon, where Taylor encountered Nana. Incredibly, Nana and his men apparently made this trip and then back over the mountains in no more than 24 hours on horseback and foot.

Or did they?

---

[113] Lekson, p. 28

Tracking Nana

Presumably the Apaches had scouted Gold Dust enough to know it was vulnerable to these tactics, but this episode still seems out of character for Nana. One can imagine him looting and burning the little camp or skirting it entirely to pick off a few isolated prospectors and miners as he passed. Certainly the Apache had a great deal of anger at the miners for despoiling their homeland. But this 19th Century drive-by shooting appears both pointless and unacceptably reckless for a canny warrior like Nana. A determined woman with a shotgun might have cost a brave man his life in an end without the honor gained in an encounter with a worthy foe.

The daring exploit does sound like the bold young Kaytennae, however, acting without the restraining guidance of the old man. These raiders were the decoys who had split off to the south in an unsuccessful attempt to draw Lt. Burnett away from support of Lt. Valois in the fight in the Cuchillo Negros two days before.

After Burnett broke off his pursuit the Indians stopped briefly at the Trujillo place, midway between Chloride and the town of Cuchillo on the road to the Rio Grande. Bentura Trujillo was 73 and so a contemporary of Nana's, and he called his little family settlement *Chiz* after Cochise, who he claimed as a close personal friend.[114] Trujillo was on

---

[114] Sierra Co. Historical Society, <u>History of Sierra County</u>, p. 49.

such good terms with the Chihenne that some Anglos thought he was part Apache himself (very unlikely, since he had been born in Alamosa, Colorado) and suspected him of selling guns and ammunition to the Indians.

For whatever reason, the hostiles did the Trujillos no harm but continued south along the eastern slope of the Black Range, leaving a trail of destruction designed to draw pursuit away from Nana and the main body on the other side of the mountains. They passed close enough to Hillsboro to rouse the populace there and a hastily organized posse rode out in pursuit, guided by the smoke from burning ranches along the way. The hostiles killed Perry Ousley and burned his ranch and then pounced on Absolom Irwin's spread west of Lake Valley. Irwin was not home, and his wife Sally escaped into the brush with her baby while the Apaches looted and burned the house, according to one account. According to another report, "Sally and their five children made a run for it. Some of them got away, but Sally was severely beaten and a baby was snatched from her arms."[115]

The Hillsboro volunteers arrived in Lake Valley the evening of August 18 to find the town filling with alarmed cowboys and miners from around the area. William Cotton's saloon was doing a booming business. The mood at

---

[115] Silva, Lee A. *"Warm Springs Apache Leader Nana,"* Wild West, December 2006.

the bar was not improved by the arrival of Abe Irwin, distraught over the loss of his wife and child, who he believed either dead in the fire or captured by the raiders.

The excited mob found a voice and a leader in George Daly, the town's most prominent citizen and – either by coincidence or through the ineffable workings of divine justice – one of the men in the territory Nana would have most wanted to kill, had he known of him at all.

One tale credits a wandering Chinese cook with the first discovery of "pure horn silver" in the hills south of Hillsboro, but it was a cowboy and sometime prospector named George Lufkin and local rancher R.D. McEvers who filed the first Lake Valley claims in the summer of 1878. News of their find drew other prospectors to the area and dozens of claims were staked. But assayed samples were disappointing, with silver content that would scarcely repay the cost of mining, shipping and refining the ore. It wasn't until Daly arrived on the scene that the boom began to pick up steam.

Daly was an associate of George D. Roberts, an unscrupulous stock promoter notorious for his role in what the *San Francisco Chronicle* called "the most gigantic and bare-faced swindle of the age," the Great Diamond Hoax of 1872, and a player in dozens of other dubious mining ventures in the West.[116]

---

[116] Milford, Homer, History of Lake Valley Mining District, New Mexico Abandoned Mine Lands Project, 2000.

Tracking Nana

Daly specialized in operating mining properties for the benefit of such speculators, manipulating current production figures and future prospects to allow the owners to either "bull" or "bear" the stock as needed to victimize unwary investors. Run out of Bodie, California, in 1879 after instigating a violent confrontation that left a man dead, Daly moved on to Leadville, Colorado, where Roberts was peddling stock in a mine that had been artfully "high graded" – worked out but left with a veneer of ore visible along the walls of the drifts to make it still appear to be a valuable property. To delay discovery of the fraud, Roberts intentionally provoked a strike that shut down the mine. As mine manager, Daly's role in this scheme was to keep the mine closed by tactics designed to inflame the situation and prevent any settlement of the strike until Roberts and his cronies had succeeded in unloading their shares in the worthless property.

After this unsavory episode, Daly traveled south to New Mexico Territory. Financed by Roberts, he bought up the most promising claims in the Lake Valley district and resold them to four new front companies that concealed Roberts' interest. While Daly took on the task of managing these properties, Roberts and his fellow conspirators back East promoted the fabulous but as yet untapped wealth of their new mines aggressively and creatively – when President Rutherford B. Hayes passed through the area in October 1880, he was persuaded to stop for lunch in the new camp, where First Lady Lucy Hayes was presented with a "silver brick" allegedly from the local mines.[117]

The promoters also recruited a prominent paleontologist, Edward Drinker Cope, as figurehead president of one and with seats on the boards of the other three companies. The most charitable explanation of Cope's unfortunate endorsement is that he was a far better fossil collector than geologist, and so even though he personally visited the site several times he somehow failed to discover what Roberts, Daly and the other principals in the scheme already knew: the hills above Lake Valley contained occasional rich pockets of silver chloride embedded in limestone like blueberries in a giant muffin, but prospects were poor for a profitable sustained mining operation.

The credulous boosterism of the *Albuquerque Journal* and other New Mexico newspapers brought a flood of hopeful miners and prospectors to the area, placer gold was found in nearby Berrenda Creek, and by the summer of 1881 there were an estimated 2,000 men scrabbling optimistically in the nearby hills.

The Apache barely tolerated the shepherds, farmers and ranchers swarming into their

---

[117] *Other than some shallow prospect holes, no actual mining activity occurred at Lake Valley until March 1881.*

homeland, but they hated the miners. To speak of gouging out your mother's flesh might have seemed a hyperbolic metaphor to white men, but to Nana and his people it was a perfectly accurate description of what they saw as a horrifying violation of their sacred ground.

Many years later, Juh's son Daklugie recalled an occasion when raiders returned to his father's camp in the Sierra Madre with the loot of a Mexican village, including a mule loaded with "the yellow and white metals that the White Eyes love." Nana warned the men that the yellow metal was sacred to Ussen; it might be picked up if found lying on the ground, but digging for it aroused the terrible wrath of the Mountain Gods. Turning a nugget in his hands so that it glittered in the firelight, the old man prophesied gloomily, "it is this stuff that will bring our people to ruin and cause us to lose first our land and then our lives." [118]

It's impossible to guess what Nana would have thought if someone could have explained to him that all the frenzied digging at Lake Valley was really nothing more than window dressing for a Gilded Age swindle, a scheme for one group of white men to steal money from other white men in cities far to the east. He would, however, soon have the opportunity to express his opinion of the miners.

---

[118] Ball, Indeh, p.10

Also newly arrived at the edge of town late that afternoon was 2d Lt. George Washington Smith, who had left Fort Cummings August 17 on patrol with 44 men of 9th Cavalry Companies "B" and "H."

When Daly angrily demanded to know why the lieutenant was not in hot pursuit of the murdering redskins, Smith might have tried to explain that his role was not to chase the hostiles but to block their escape.

Smith left Fort Cummings before Col. Hatch arrived, but his telegraphed orders contained enough information for the lieutenant to grasp his commander's intent. And like every other officer and man in the 9th, he probably recognized by now how futile and dangerous it was to try to track Apaches without Indian guides. Valois and Burnett with Co. "I," together with Cooley's "A" Co. and Lt. Taylor with Navajo scouts and part of "B" and "H," were sweeping down through the Black Range, driving Nana and his war party before them. Smith and his men were part of the cordon Hatch was throwing across southwestern New Mexico to catch the raiders when they were flushed out of the mountains.

The lieutenant was no West Point shavetail but an old soldier, a Civil War veteran who had ended that war a Lt. Colonel and had spent the past eight years fighting Indians; he probably recognized the hoorawing of Gold Dust and the smoke of the burning ranches as a diversion. If the hostiles were laying a clear trail it was because they wanted the soldiers to chase them.

Rather than try to explain military strategy to a crowd of belligerent drunks, however, Smith fell back on protesting that his men and horses were worn out and in need of a rest before continuing the chase. But when Daly announced he would lead his saloon regulators after the Indians with or without the soldiers, Smith reluctantly agreed to mount up.[119] He took 16 men – perhaps all that had serviceable horses at that point – and Sgt. Brent Woods, leaving First Sgt. Richard Anderson at Lake Valley in charge of the rest of the command, presumably with strict orders to keep the troopers out of Cotton's Saloon, and led out sometime after midnight.

The trail led west along Berrenda Creek, across Macho Canyon and up Pollock Canyon and then over the crest of the Mimbres Mountains down into Dry Gavilan Canyon.[120] About 10 o'clock on the morning of August 19, after a long night in the saddle, Smith called a halt. Surveying the terrain ahead, he hesitated

---

[119] *It could be that both civilians and soldiers were influenced by concern for the missing Sally Irwin, who wouldn't turn up in town with her baby, footsore but otherwise unharmed, until the next day.*

[120] *There's some difference of opinion as to whether the ambush occurred in Dry Gavilan Canyon or Pollack Canyon. A local rancher tells me he's found old .45-70 brass in the rocks above Pollack Canyon.*

to venture any farther without first scouting the heights on either side. Perhaps he had already heard about Captain Parker's defeat in Carrizo Canyon, or he was simply canny enough to sniff a trap before he put his foot in it.

Half the civilian volunteers had dropped out during the hard night's ride as Cotton's whisky wore off, but Daly was still in the hunt with about 20 followers. Riding up to the head of the column, he angrily upbraided the lieutenant for his timidity and may have impugned that officer's courage and that of his soldiers. Those would have been hard words to hear for a man who had fought at Chickamauga and was now doing a dirty, dangerous job in his country's service for far less money than this blustering civilian was making peddling watered mining stock. And as it happened, Lt. Smith was risking his life for free that day. He was under stoppage of pay for some irregularity in his accounts, and before he left Fort Cummings he had penned an appeal to the Army bean-counters to at least place him on half-pay so he could support his wife and daughter.

For whatever reason Smith let Daly's bullying over-ride his own better judgment it was a fatal mistake for both men. Whether it was Kaytennae or Nana in person laying the ambush, he knew his business. The hostiles waited until the column was well into the defile before opening fire, and their first volley was aimed at the leaders in front and the pack mules bringing up the rear to trap the soldiers and their allies in the kill zone. Daly was one of the first killed in the fusillade from the cliffs above and Smith was hit and knocked from the saddle. As he was being helped back on his horse he was struck again and killed. The panicked posse fled, colliding with the pack train coming down the narrow canyon behind them, and horses, men and mules dissolved into a chaotic tangle under the murderous fire.

With Smith dead command devolved upon Sergeant Woods. According to his Medal of Honor citation, the 35-year-old Woods "by his coolness, bravery, and unflinching devotion to duty in standing by his commanding officer in an exposed position under a heavy fire from a large party of Indians saved the lives of at least three of his comrades."

Woods extricated the survivors from the canyon but was forced to leave behind his dead, as well as 30 horses and pack mules loaded with 1,000 rounds of ammunition. While most of the posse didn't stop running until they reached Lake Valley, Woods regrouped his troopers and the remaining civilians behind the rocky outcrops scattered on the saddle of the pass. From there he held the hostiles off until Sgt. Anderson arrived that afternoon with the remainder of the detachment to relieve him.

The lieutenant and three troopers – Privates Thomas Golding (Kühn gives the name as Giddings), James Brown and Monroe

Overstreet – were killed. Pvt. William Hollins survived a bullet through the lungs but received a medical discharge five months later, Pvt. John William was shot in the thigh and eventually lost his leg, and Pvt. Wesley Harris was shot in the right breast.[121] Daly and at least one other civilian were killed and seven or eight others wounded in the six-hour firefight.

According to one account, "small pools of blood in the canyon battlefield indicated that at least a few of the warriors had been killed or wounded."

"Daly was found shot four or five times and mutilated, with sticks stuck into his body. Smith was found lying on his face with his back and arms burnt. His face had been slashed, with his nose, ears and other body parts cut off. The lieutenant's mustache was found hanging in a nearby bush." [122]

Moving down Gavilan Canyon, Anderson and Woods met up with Captain Bryan Dawson and Lt. Eugene Dimmick with the rest of Companies "B" and "H" and Lt. Taylor and his company of Navajo scouts.[123] Dawson sent the

---

[121] *According to Sheridan* (Record of Engagements, p. 115) *Lt. Smith and four men were killed.*

[122] Silva, Lee A. *"Warm Springs Apache Leader Nana,"* Wild West, December 2006.

[123] *Eugene Dumont Dimmick served with both the 5th NY Cavalry and the Veteran's Reserve Corps during the Civil War and with the 5th, 9th and 10th Cavalry during the Indian Wars. In 1890 he was brevetted Captain for gallant and meritorious service in action against the Indians in the Black Range on*

casualties back to Fort Bayard, where Sgt. George Turpin delivered the sad news to Lt. Smith's widow.[124]

She may have escorted her husband's coffin back east for burial, but given her financial straits it's possible he is buried in the national cemetery at Silver City. Daly was presumably laid to rest in the new cemetery at Lake Valley, although his grave is unmarked today.

On Friday, August 19, the same day as the fight in Gavilan Canyon, Apaches surprised a party of Hispanic woodcutters in their camp near Mule Springs, a few miles from Fort Cummings. "Desadario Hereda and Patronillo Chacon were killed at the camp, and Manuel and Juan Chacon, lads of twelve and fourteen years of age, are supposed to have been carried off prisoners, as their bodies could not be found."[125] Four men were killed, according to another account, which added that: "In Las Cruces, Apaches attacked a wagon, killing six Mexicans and severely wounding the lone survivor." [126]

The next evening two men were killed by Apaches near Eureka, a small mining camp in the Little Hatchet Mountains in the New Mexico Bootheel.[127]

September 23, 1879.
[124] Kenner, p. 230.
[125] *Silver City Chronicle*, August 25, 1881.
[126] Silva, *"Warm Springs Apache Leader Nana,"* <u>Wild West</u>, December 2006

The ambush in Gavilan Canyon had blown a hole in Col. Hatch's cordon between the mountains and the border. The soldiers who should have been blocking Nana's movement south were left far behind him, short on horses and ammunition. Nana passed eight miles west of Fort Cummings, probably on the night of August 20, and rode on into the Florida Mountains, crossing into Mexico two or three days later.[128]

---

[127] Kühn, p. 247.

[128] *If there were still Navajo or Mescalero warriors with the main party, they may have turned back northeast (which would account for a final attack near Las Cruces) and made their way back to their respective reservations.*

9

The Aftermath

'Revenge is a kind of wild justice.' – Francis Bacon

According to one report, four Hispanic shepherds were killed in the San Mateos on August 31. A posse of 15 men from Fairview (Winston) and Chloride "took the trail in search of the savages but apparently never caught up with them."[129]

As Nana was already in Mexico by that time, these murders may have been committed by a spinoff from his war party, perhaps Navajo or Mescalero on their way back to their own reservations. Or they may have been the work of white men. Together with miners and prospectors, the flood of longhorns moving into the territory brought with it some of the roughest elements of the Texas frontier, men who would have thought little of killing an unarmed *pastor* in cold blood. (Elfego Baca had his own dealings with them in nearby Frisco, Magdalena and Socorro.)[130]

On September 25, more than a month after Nana and his men crossed the border, Plácida and her nephew Procópio escaped their captors

---

[129] Looney, Ralph. Haunted Highways, p. 151.

[130] Silva, Lee A. *"Elfego Baca; Forgotten Fighter for Law and Order,"* in America,, The Men and Their Guns That Made Her Great, Craig Boddington, ed., Los Angeles, 1981, pp. 93-115.

while the Apaches were skirmishing with Mexican irregulars during a horse-stealing raid in Chihuahua. The Mexicans escorted the two fugitives to the border at Ysleta, Texas, where a kindly family took them in until Plácida's brother and other men from Cubero came down to take them home. Shortly afterwards she married Victor Romero, one of the men who had brought her back from Texas, and bore another daughter who had been fathered by one of Nana's warriors or perhaps by Nana himself.

Although she claimed to know the names of the Navajo men who had murdered her husband and kidnapped her daughter, they were never brought to justice and she never succeeded in recovering little Trinidad. To fulfill a vow she made to *Señora de la Luz*[131] during her captivity, Plácida composed an *indita* (a traditional New Mexican folk ballad similar in structure to the Mexican *corrido*) telling of her ordeal and miraculous escape.[132]

Other captives were eventually recovered as well. In August 1883 Jose Maria Madrid traveled to San Carlos from his home in Quemado looking for his son Martin, who had been captured in Nana's raid. A year later Madrid and a companion returned to the

---

[131] *The Iglesia de Nuestra Señora de la Luz is a classic Hispanic church built in 1881 in nearby Cañoncito.*
[132] Roland, ed. *"The Ballad of Placida Romero,"* <u>New Mexico Historical Review</u>, Summer 2011, p. 300.

reservation to reclaim a second son and another boy. Two more New Mexican boys, one taken in Nana's raid and the other during the Victorio War, were also given up by the Chiricahua that fall.[133]

Col. Edward Hatch never did get his general's star. In his report to Gen. John Pope, commander of the Department of the Missouri, Hatch cited the multiple difficulties imposed by the terrain, the weather, and the frustrating ease with which his quarry scattered and slipped out of his grasp. "(I)t can be truly said that the troops did everything that was possible, and pressed the Indians so closely and persistently from so many directions that they had no time to rest, and finally were driven across the Mexican line," Hatch wrote.

Valid as these excuses were, there was no denying that one old man and his small band of followers had rampaged across New Mexico and escaped back across the border apparently unscathed, and many in the territory were wondering not if but when the raiders would return in greater numbers. In passing Hatch's report on to General Sherman in Washington, Pope praised the colonel for his "well-known activity and gallantry," asserting that in the pursuit of Nana Hatch "did all that man could do and is entitled to high consideration for and acknowledgement of his services." But Pope went on to say (accurately) that the 9th was

[133] Sweeney, <u>From Cochise to Geronimo</u>, pp. 380-81.

"run down in men and horses," and "entitled to some rest, which I hope to give them this winter."[134]

Hatch and his regiment were transferred to Fort Riley, Kansas, by the end of the year and replaced by Col. Ranald S. Mackenzie and his 4th Cavalry.[135]

Nana returned to the fastness of the Sierra Madre where the band's women and children were waiting, perhaps shepherded by Lozen, who had by then returned from her own solo odyssey to the Mescalero Reservation. When his warriors recited their exploits around the fire, the Apaches agreed that Nana had earned his place among the greatest.

"I believe Nana was responsible for more deaths than either Geronimo or Victorio," Kaywaykla said many years later. "But we did not have the mania for statistics that White Eyes do, and did not count the dead. Usen (sic) had not commanded that we love our enemies. Nana did not love his; and he was not content with an eye for an eye, nor a life for a life. For every Apache killed he took many lives."[136]

---

[134] Lincoln, Robert T. Annual Report of the Secretary of War for the Year 1881, Vol.I, p. 118.

[135] *Hatch, 57, died from injuries sustained in a buckboard accident at Fort Robinson, Nebraska, in 1889. Possibly spooked by a rattlesnake, his team stampeded and the colonel was tangled in the reins and dragged some distance.*

[136] Ball, In the Days of Victorio, pp 119-120

No one knows the true final tally of Nana's Raid. Based on the newspaper and military reports I have seen, I calculate the raiders killed 8 soldiers and 64 civilians, wounded 10 soldiers and 15 civilians, and captured 14 civilians. There were other deaths that never made their way into newspaper accounts or official reports. Lone prospectors, shepherds and other wanderers in the mountains and deserts may have simply disappeared without trace, their scattered bones only discovered years later. A reasonable guess would be more than 100 dead, wounded and missing/captured in the five weeks from July 17 to August 20, making Nana's Raid a bloodier affray than Pancho Villa's raid 35 years later.[137]

Although officers reported "pools of blood" on the field and in one case "a number of bodies … concealed among the rocks," the Indians never admitted to any casualties among the raiding party.

There was no one else in the Sierra Madres to join in Nana's victory dance. The Chokonen, under Cochise's son Naiche (Nachez), with Juh and his Nednhis (the Southern Chiricahua band the Mexicans knew as the Bronco Apaches because of their wild intractability), were on the San Carlos Reservation in Arizona that summer, together with Loco, Chatto,

---

[137] *Eight soldiers and 10 civilians were killed in Villa's attack on the border town of Columbus, N.M., in 1916.*

Mangas, the remainder of the Chihenne, the Bedonkhe under Chihuahua, and Geronimo, who was rapidly assembling his own following.

Word of Nana's exploits had already reached the reservation before Chihuahua and the rest of his company returned after their discharge from the Scouts. On August 11, two days after the raid on Garcia, General Orlando B. Willcox,[138] commander of the Department of Arizona, telegraphed Col. Eugene A. Carr,[139] who was at Fort Apache with two companies of his 6th Cavalry, "to hold his command in readiness to take the field, as Hatch reports approach of hostiles from New Mexico."

But the real trouble was brewing among the Western Apaches. Cousins but never close friends of the Chiricahua, the White Mountain, Coyotero and Tonto Apaches had been pacified by Crook's first Arizona campaign in 1872-'73 and had given little trouble since. But the stress of consolidating thousands of Indians at San Carlos and Fort Apache in the 1870s resulted in feuding and dissension between the

---

[138] *An 1843 graduate of West Point, Willcox rose to Major General of Volunteers in the Civil War and held the regular Army brevet rank of Brigadier General in 1881.*
[139] *A West Pointer who fought Apaches before the Civil War, Carr was awarded the Congressional Medal of Honor and rose to the brevet rank of Major General in that conflict. Reverting to his regular Army rank, he served first against the Cheyenne and then the Apache before retiring as Brigadier General in 1892. He died in 1910 at age 70.*

various bands and anger and dissatisfaction with the authorities.

In the summer of 1881 the White Mountain Apaches at Cibecue, northwest of Fort Apache, found a messiah in the person of a charismatic shaman called Noche-del-klinne (Nakaidoklini, Nakadoklini, Nock-ay-det-klinne), who whites called "The Dreamer" or "the Doctor." In June, at the same time Nana was preparing his foray north from Mexico, Noche-del-klinne began preaching a mystical vision that promised salvation to the demoralized Apaches. His message was almost identical to that of Wodziwob, a prophet who began proselytizing the Paiute in Nevada a decade earlier: if the People danced, if they prayed, if they *believed,* the hairy, pale-eyed people would disappear and their revered dead chiefs would return to life. The Dreamer prophesied this would come to pass "when the corn was ripe."[140]

Wodziwob's eschatological cult had died out among the Paiute by 1881 (it would be revived by Wovoka, another prophet, later in the decade and spread east to the Sioux with tragic consequences) but the message found a receptive audience among the Apaches in Arizona in the summer of 1881.[141]

---

[140]Willcox, O.B., in Annual Report of the Secretary of War for the Year 1881, p. 153.
[141] *Aleshire refers to the Apache winter season as the "Ghost Dance" and Sweeney calls those months the "Ghost Face." I don't know that the Apaches called the Dreamer's ceremonies a*

Tracking Nana

Before embarking on his raid in July, Nana traveled secretly up from Mexico to observe the ceremonies and form his own opinion of the medicine man. According to Juh's son Asa Daklugie, who was a boy on the reservation at the time, to prove his power to the skeptical Chiricahuas Noche-del-klinne (briefly) conjured up the spirits of Cochise, Mangas Coloradas and Victorio. "Nana said that he had seen this and the word of Nana was not to be questioned," Daklugie said.[142]

Despite his endorsement of the Dreamer's Power, Nana returned to Mexico, where he was pursuing his own plan to make the whites disappear, and few Chiricahua joined the cult.

Whether Noche-del-klinne was promising the whites would die, go back where they came from, or simply disappear was never clear to the nervous agent and the Army officers, but they were certain the movement represented some kind of defiance to their authority. Col. Carr was especially worried about his Apache scouts, most of whom were if not followers of the Dreamer at least respectful of his Power. On August 13 Carr ordered their commander, 2d Lt. Thomas Cruse, to collect his men's arms due to "their disposition to treachery."[143]

"ghost dance," but the similarities to the Paiute religious revival are clear. The very idea of raising the dead was contrary to traditional Apache beliefs.
[142] Bell, Indeh, p.54.
[143] Carr to Wilcox, Aug. 17, 1881, quoted in Annual Report of

Carr received a telegram from Willcox that same day directing him to arrest the shaman if the agent, Joseph C. Tiffany, concurred. When Carr asked his opinion, Tiffany responded, "I want him arrested or killed, or both."[144] That left Carr in a quandary: he needed his scouts to accomplish this mission, but he didn't trust them. He temporized for two weeks and then, apparently reasoning that if the scouts were disposed to make trouble they would at least wait until after payday to rebel or desert, he returned their guns and on August 30 took 23 Apache scouts, 5 officers and 79 soldiers up to Cibecue to arrest the Dreamer. In the confrontation that followed the scouts turned on the soldiers, the prophet was killed by his guards and six troopers and an officer were killed in the melee.[145]

The angry Apaches followed Carr's battered force back to Fort Apache and attacked the post. By the time they were driven off, Carr's losses totaled 10 dead and wounded, with another 6 civilians killed in the area.

Juh and Geronimo were involved in the fighting as well as Lozen, according to Daklugie, but Nana is not mentioned. It's improbable but not impossible he was present,

---

the Secretary of War, 1881, p. 142.

[144] Collins, Charles. Apache Nightmare: The Battle at Cibecue Creek, p. 24.

[145] Lincoln, Robert T. Annual Report of the Secretary of War, 1881, p.143.

since he had crossed into Mexico 10 days previously and conceivably might have immediately turned around and re-crossed the border into Arizona.

The first news Gen. Willcox received at Prescott was a wildly exaggerated report that Carr "had been attacked, his command exterminated and, subsequently, Fort Apache taken."[146] With the telegraph lines cut, the Gila River in flood and the roads washed out by the summer's heavy rains, Carr was out of communication and temporarily beyond aid. In Washington, General Sherman was outraged by the resulting newspaper headlines coming on top of the complaints he had been receiving for the past two months of Apache depredations in New Mexico. "I want this annual Apache stampede to end right now, and to effect that result will send every available man in the whole Army if necessary," he wired Gen. Irvin McDowell, commander of the Department of California, in San Francisco Sept. 16.[147]

The General of the Army's displeasure over-rode the bureaucratic boundaries of the Military Districts of Arizona and New Mexico, and Gen. Pope immediately ordered the commander of Fort Wingate to take his garrison and march west toward Arizona. Col. Mackenzie, who had just finished settling the Utes on their new reservation in Colorado, was

---

[146] Ibid, p. 140.
[147] Ibid, p. 144.

ordered to bring six companies of his 4th Cavalry down to New Mexico by rail, march west to catch up to the Fort Wingate force, and then continue on to relieve Fort Apache. In the meantime, Willcox got additional troops moving to the scene from the south.

The arrival of all these soldiers alarmed the Chiricahuas, who were warned by two of the White Mountain rebel leaders that the troops were going to attack the Chiricahua camps. On Sept. 30, Juh and Geronimo, accompanied by Naiche, Chatto and Chihuahua, fled the reservation with 74 men and their women and children to join Nana and his people in the Sierra Madre. Not all the Chiricahua left, however, and six months later Geronimo re-crossed the border and slipped onto the reservation to round up Loco's band and escort them back to Mexico. With that exodus the Chihenne were finally reunited, but their homeland was lost beyond redemption.

When the Texas Pacific, building west from San Antonio, connected with the Southern Pacific and the A.T. & S.F. in the fall of 1881, the Americans had secured their claim to Apachería with bands of steel. The mining boom in the Black Range and Mogollons picked up steam as declining production on the Comstock Lode in Nevada drew experienced miners and prospectors as well as Eastern investors to new opportunities in the Southwest. The economic effects of the Panic of 1873 lingered for more than a decade and the weak economy left tens of thousands of working men unemployed or underemployed. For the boldest of those the new railroads offered a fast and relatively inexpensive route to new opportunities in the West.

"The reports from our mining districts are so encouraging as to lead thousands of prospectors into the mountains from the North, South, East and West," the *Journal* enthused.[148]

"In southwestern New Mexico, prospectors swarmed over every mountain and hill in search of silver. Spurred on by reports of successful mining at Chloride Flat and Georgetown, they combed every inch of accessible land, and many new prospects were uncovered," according to mining historian Paige Christiansen. "The scene was set: gold and silver mines were a reality; prospectors had located what were described as fabulous ore bodies; speculators were touting New Mexico as the richest mining area in the United States; and foreign and domestic investors began to respond as gold and silver bullion began to flow out of New Mexico in the late 1870s, ushering in the most romantic, the most exciting, the most lawless, and certainly the wildest period in the history of mining in New Mexico."[149]

Over the next decade the railroads thrust tendrils into the mountains from the south and

---

[148] *Albuquerque Daily Journal*, Dec. 8, 1880.

[149] Christiansen, Paige W. The Story of Mining in New Mexico, pp. 55-56.

east. The grandly-named Silver City, Deming & Pacific connected with the Southern Pacific in 1883, and the next year the Santa Fe completed a branch line to Lake Valley and another to Magdalena. The population of the Territory grew by nearly a third between 1870 and 1880 and by another third from 1880 to 1890.

"When I first saw a railway train – a solid example of the white man's magic – I began to see," an old Kiowa wrote years later. "The world moves faster than men – and it moves for the white men only."

Down in Mexico Nana aligned himself with Geronimo, the most obdurate and belligerent of the surviving leaders. In March 1883 there was another bloody foray across the border, this time led by Chatto. The raiders captured the nation's attention by murdering a Silver City mining promoter, Judge Hamilton C. McComas, and his wife Juniata and carrying off their six-year-old son Charley. The little boy's angelic Victorian portrait tugged at the public heartstrings and increased pressure on Gen. Crook to recover the boy and end the Apache menace once and for all.

Crook had developed the formula for success: Apache scouts, led by a few intrepid young officers and supported by mule trains carrying supplies where no wagon could penetrate. All that stood in his way were the international boundary and his own sympathy for his Apache opponents.

That first obstacle was overcome by Mexican dictator Porfirio Diaz, who was prepared to overlook old grievances if it helped him exert control over his troublesome northern frontier. He had enlisted ex-bandits as *Rurales* to chase bandits, and he was prepared to use the U.S. Cavalry to fight Apaches if he had to. In July 1882 the Mexican government concluded an agreement with the Americans allowing for "hot pursuit" of raiders across the international boundary, and Crook seized on the McComas tragedy to justify plunging into northern Mexico with his Apache scouts.

On May 1, 1883, the general crossed the border in person with nearly 200 Apache scouts under white officers, backed by a company of cavalry and supported by a well-provisioned mule train. Two weeks later, the scouts surprised Chihuahua's *rancheriá* in the foothills of the Sierra Madre and fell on it without parley. They killed between four and nine people and captured five more, thus demonstrating that they – and Crook – were in deadly earnest. Crook released two of the captured women to carry his message to the hostiles: the general was in the mountains to fight, and he had brought plenty of bullets. They must either fight him or give up.

Crook never did find little Charley or recover his body[150] but in June 1883, Nana and Loco

---

[150] *Rumors persisted that the boy was still alive and years later some claimed he was leading a band of renegade Apaches, but*

with a handful of followers turned themselves in and were escorted north to San Carlos. Nana probably came in first to test whether Crook's word was good and there would be no repercussions from past crimes before the rest committed themselves. Geronimo and the other holdouts came in some months later.

So Nana was in the place he had struggled to avoid for the past ten years, on San Carlos Reservation. Some tried to adapt – Chatto joined the Scouts as sergeant, and Chihuahua re-enlisted – but most found little to do but sit around in idleness. Lt. Britton Davis, the agent they derisively nicknamed "Fat Boy," nagged at them to try farming, but scratching in the dirt was no work for a man. The women grew sullen working in the sun and so had to be disciplined. And then Fat Boy complained they were beating their wives!

There was a woman with them highly skilled in the making of tiswin, and it could be some were spiking the mildly alcoholic corn brew with whiskey smuggled onto the reservation by unscrupulous traders. Whatever the reason, "tiswin parties" degenerated from convivial gatherings to drunken brawls, and Crook had ordered them stopped. Defying this ban, Geronimo hosted a tiswin drunk at his camp on May 14, 1885. Nursing their grievances around the fire, Nana and the others decided

---

it seems certain he was killed by an enraged warrior within a few weeks of his capture.

they would all go down to the agent's tent the next morning and have it out with him. The Fat Boy's *calabozo* wasn't big enough to hold them all if they stuck together, they reassured each other.

Britt Davis may have been a little overweight, but he was a brave man. Facing dozens of angry and defiant Apaches, most either still drunk or nursing mean hangovers and at least some of them armed, he was conciliatory but noncommittal. Falling back on the bureaucrat's standard defense, he told the Indians he would forward their complaints to Crook and the general would decide what was to be done. Meanwhile, Davis suggested, they should all go back to their wickiups and sleep it off.

Crook probably could have defused the situation by coming to San Carlos in person and playing his celebrated solo good cop-bad cop routine, alternately listening sympathetically to the malcontents and berating them like naughty children before an angry grandparent. As they sobered up at least half the protestors were already sorry they had pushed so hard, and all were wondering what Crook would have to say. But the general never got the message.[151]

---

[151] *Archie McIntosh, Crook's chief scout and trusted Indian advisor, was himself too hungover to recognize the significance of the message. He rolled over and went back to sleep, and the vital telegram was pigeonholed en route.*

Tracking Nana

Geronimo, Nana and the rest sat around uneasily for the next two days like schoolboys waiting in the principal's office. They were only too aware that the vast majority of settlers and most of the soldiers wanted the Chiricahua gone from Arizona altogether, preferably to hell but at least as far as Indian Territory in any event. Finally deciding that if he was silent so long Crook must be planning some terrible punishment, Geronimo, Nana, Mangas, Chihuahua and Naiche fled once again into the Sierra Madre.

The rest of the story is too grim to be repeated here more than very briefly. Crook enlisted more Scouts, now including Chatto with some of his and Loco's men, and sent them in pursuit. For years Pope and other Army officers had been arguing that the only way to bring peace to the border was to round up all the Apaches and ship them far away, and the Chiricahua still on the reservation were afraid that drastic course would be adopted if Geronimo and his followers were not suppressed once and for all. These men knew all the trails and refuges in the Sierra, and in June, a little more than a month after the breakout, the Scouts surprised Chihuahua and Ulzana's camp and captured their families. In August they surprised Geronimo's *ranchería* even deeper in the Sierra Madre, capturing three of his wives and five of his children as well as Nana's own wife. The leaders and most of their warriors escaped, but the loss of their families was a heavy blow.

In November 1885 the hostiles struck back. Chihuahua launched a raid into southwestern New Mexico as a diversion while his brother Ulzana made a bold attempt to liberate their families in Arizona. Chihuahua reached as far north as the vicinity of Lake Valley and the Mimbres Mountains before retiring back across the border. Ulzana stayed longer and did much more damage. Balked in the attempted rescue of their families, he and his men attacked a White Mountain camp on the reservation, killing 21 men, women and children in retaliation for their collaboration with the Army. The raiders then ambushed a pursuing cavalry column, killing five soldiers before escaping back to Mexico. With the ranchers, cowboys and random travelers killed along their route, the death toll from this raid was probably about 40 people.

Nana was also reported back in the Mogollons about this time,[152] but didn't linger. The mountains were full of white people, Territorial Gov. Lionel Sheldon had authorized local communities to form their own militia companies to hunt Indians, and the soldiers were again encamped at Ojo Caliente, blocking access to the sacred spring.

On March 27, 1886, Geronimo, Chihuahua, and Nana met Crook just south of the Arizona

---

[152] Utley, Geronimo, p. 173.

border in the *Cañon de los Embudos* to negotiate their surrender. A famous photograph taken on that occasion shows Nana seated close behind Geronimo at the peace talk. (Years later, Geronimo would say that if he had listened to his old *compadre* he never would have given up.) While Nana came in as promised, Geronimo got drunk and bolted at the last minute in what proved to be the final disaster for the tribe. Crook resigned and was replaced by Gen. Nelson Miles, a hard war man after Sheridan's own heart, who was prepared to implement the final solution: all the Chiricahua, hostile and friendly, were to be removed.

On April 8, Nana left Fort Bowie with 74 other Chiricahua as prisoners of war. They would be held first in Florida, then in Alabama and finally at Fort Sill, Oklahoma, for the next 27 years. Nana never again saw his beloved mountains, or the sacred spring at Ojo Caliente. He died in Oklahoma in 1896.

Epilogue

*"Nothing lives long except the earth and
the mountains." – Cheyenne death song*[153]

The miners took millions of dollars' worth of
gold and silver out of the mountains of
southwestern New Mexico over the next 20
years. While the early reports are tainted by
local boosterism, aggressive stock jobbing and
fraud, it's estimated the Mogollon District
yielded $5 million, Magdalena nearly $9
million, Hillsboro $6 million and Silver City's
Chloride Flats $4 million by 1900. Just one
property, the *Naiad Queen* north of Santa Rita,
produced $3 million by the end of the century
and the *Bridal Chamber* at Lake Valley claimed
$8 million, while the placer deposits at nearby
Gold Dust are said to have yielded more than
$2 million before they were worked out.

Although 19th Century miners rarely if ever
paused to reckon the environmental cost, it
was high. Cooney's *Silver Bar*, for example,
required between 100,000 and 150,000 feet of
timber to produce $1.7 million worth of ore.
Clear cutting the nearby slopes led to flash
floods that ultimately swept the little town
away altogether. Mogollon, Silver City,
Hillsboro and other mining camps suffered

---

[153] Brandon, William. The American Heritage Book of Indians,
p. 324.

similar devastating floods – call it the revenge of the Mountain Gods.

And while the gold was real enough the silver was a sort of Gilded Age fairy gold, the market price subsidized by the government. When that prop was knocked out in the 1890s most of the mines closed down and the little towns emptied almost as quickly as they had sprung up. Silver City still thrives today as a college town and retirement community, and the hills around Lake Valley have been subdivided into 40-acre ranchettes. But Hillsboro, Magdalena, Winston and Mogollon just barely hang on, while Grafton, Cooley, Eureka and other camps have disappeared altogether.

Mining was dirty and dangerous work, and no one but a romantic who hasn't tried it would mourn its passing. The miners left behind some colorful names that would delight the ear of Stephen Vincent Benét – the *Happy Jack* and *Last Chance*, the *Mountain King*, *Miner's Dream*, *Ready Pay*, *Golden Opportunity* and dozens of others -- now fading away on the yellowing paper of old stock certificates. The miners' enduring monument is Cooney's Tomb,[154] their legacy thousands of abandoned diggings in the back country. Of the 3,000 known

---

[154] *An ex-cavalry sergeant who made the first big strike in the Mogollons, James Cooney was killed by Victorio's Apaches in 1880. His brother interred him in a crypt carved into a massive boulder in the canyon near his mine.*

hardrock mines in New Mexico, fewer than 100 have been inventoried or surveyed to date.

The Buffalo Soldiers are memorialized by a martial statue standing on the weed-grown parade ground of old Fort Bayard near Silver City. A bronze plaque recalls the nine black enlisted men and two white officers of the 9th Cavalry who were awarded the Medal of Honor for their service in a hard and dirty war. They were little appreciated in their day, either by the people of New Mexico or the Army.

The cows are still on the land, although not in the numbers that grazed the range in the last quarter of the 19th Century. Between 1882 and 1884 the number of cattle in Socorro County, which then included what's now Sierra County, exploded from 9,000 to more than 70,000 head. In recent years the government has been steadily reducing the herds on public lands, and the small ranchers who depend on those grazing permits are increasingly marginalized. But ranching today, like 19th Century silver mining, depends on a government subsidy. In 2014 the BLM spent $34 million administering grazing leases but collected just $12 million in fees, and political support for that imbalance is waning. The federal agencies that control the land are less responsive to the dwindling numbers of ranchers on the land than to urban environmentalists who have never seen a calf disemboweled by a wolf but value wildlife over hamburger on the hoof.

Tracking Nana

And in southwestern New Mexico the feds call the tune. The Gila National Forest encompasses 3.3 million acres, about a quarter of it protected wilderness, while Cibola NF covers another 1.6 million acres, 63,000 of it in the Apache Kid and Withington Wilderness. Catron County is the largest in the state in area but one of the least populated; 80 percent of the land is owned by federal or state government. In neighboring Sierra County three-quarters of the land is controlled by various federal agencies.

After years of legal battles the descendants of the Chiricahuas exiled in 1886, now known as the Fort Sill Apaches, have won recognition as a New Mexico tribe, together with a tiny reservation that consists of nothing more than a smoke shop on Interstate 10 near Deming. Most of the tribe's 700 members live in Lawton, Oklahoma, or on the Mescalero Reservation.

A few never left. There were bronco Apaches high in the Sierra Madre as late as the 1930s, and at least one renegade roamed the New Mexico and Arizona mountains until 1906, when a posse killed Massai deep in the San Mateos.

The sacred spring still flows, not many miles from Massai's grave. I've been told there are rattlers up there active all winter long, perhaps because the water warms the ground around the spring. I'd like to believe they remember Nana's Power and have been set there as sentinels to warn away trespassers.

Tracking Nana

Nana was a brilliant tactician who took full advantage of two of the Apaches' great strengths in irregular warfare: their incredible stamina and their ability to travel rapidly over rough country on foot and horseback. By splitting up, moving fast and striking at widely separated points in quick succession, the raiders mitigated their disadvantage in numbers. Unsure where his opponents were and confused by conflicting reports, Hatch was forced to divide his cavalry into small detachments in order to cover all possible options. As a result the Apaches enjoyed a parity or even superiority of numbers in every engagement.

Nana had several objectives in the raid. The first was to avenge the death of Victorio and the others killed at Tres Castillos, and he succeeded in this. Other raids followed, led by Chatto, Ulzana, Chihuahua and Geronimo, but none matched Nana's body count.

His second objective was in the nature of a religious pilgrimage. Nana was determined to visit the Chihenne holy places, and in this he was less successful. After pausing at Salinas Peak he made three attempts to reach Ojo Caliente – once when he crossed the river near Elephant Butte but instead diverted up into the San Mateos, again when he challenged the cavalry at Cuchillo Negro, and finally when he encountered Lt. Taylor in Whitehorse Canyon. Thwarted on each occasion, he may have slipped back across the border during Ulzana's raid in the fall of 1885 to make one last try.

At one time I thought of this element of the raid as an old man's farewell tour, made in the expectation he would never again see the sacred mountain or soak his aching bones in the healing water of the warm spring before he died. Now I believe I underestimated the old man's stubborn determination. Nana was not surrendering to fate but gathering his strength for the struggle to come. Far from giving up, he was determined to fight on.

His third objective on the raid was to gather arms and ammunition to continue the war, and with the capture of the cavalry's pack mules in Gavilan Canyon, he once again displayed his Power over ammunition.

Whether his raid was also part of a broader strategic plan is a tantalizing question.

"From the white point of view, the wild ride seemed senseless – a fusillade of destruction wrought by Indians who had no strategic aim save terror, no land or rights to win," according to Roberts.[155] But Nana did have one conversation with a white man in which he clearly stated his goal and how he hoped to achieve it. When he talked with Robert Stapleton in the San Mateos after the ambush in Red Canyon, Stapleton asked what he wanted to end his war. Nana replied that if the Ojo Caliente Reservation were re-established

---

[155] Roberts, <u>Once They Moved Like the Wind</u>, p.195.

and all the Chihenne allowed to return there, he would be willing to surrender. If not, he would fight on to the end. And he even told Stapleton how he intended to do that: he was going north to the Navajo country

Nana's Raid, like Lee's Gettysburg Campaign, may have been a final throw of the dice against steadily worsening odds.

Before he embarked on his raid, Nana surreptitiously visited the San Carlos reservation to attend Noche-del-klinne's "ghost dance" ceremonies. He apparently came away convinced that the White Mountain prophet's Power was genuine. Juh, Geronimo and Kaytennae were also persuaded.[156]

Although the official consensus was that the Cibecue attack was a spontaneous explosion ignited by Col. Carr's mishandling of a delicate situation, some at the time believed the uprising was planned well in advance. Army officers at Fort Apache and civilians at the Agency all heard disquieting rumors circulating on the reservation that summer. Weeks before Nana's raiders reached the southern borders of the Navajo Reservation, San Carlos Agent Tiffany heard that a Navajo had visited the White Mountain camps, urging them to take the warpath. At about the same time, Noche-del-klinne began telling his followers that he would not be able to raise their dead chiefs and relatives until *after* the white men left the

---

[156] Ball, Indeh, pp. 53-54.

country. The implication was clear: the Apaches must do more than pray, they must act.

When Lt. Cruse, the commander of the Indian scout company at Fort Apache, sent Sam Bowman, his chief of scouts, to Cibecue, the lieutenant "was shocked when the man came back offering his resignation, full of dire predictions of a mass outbreak."[157]

On August 7 a party of about 30 Navajo arrived at San Carlos with blankets they wanted to trade with the reservation Indians, and Agent Tiffany heard they were bartering for cartridges.[158]

Although the Apaches were a frustrating problem, it was the far more numerous Navajo who really worried General Pope. In his 1881 report, he nervously estimated the Navajo could field 3,000 warriors, "a most formidable force in those mountains, and one which would require a very heavy force of troops to deal with," and warned that they were seriously discontented. "Whilst things may drift on for a time at the Navajo Agency without open trouble, I am entirely satisfied that there is danger all the time of serious difficulty."[159]

And neighboring the Navajo to the north were the Ute. Their uprising was less than two years past, and only the presence of Mackenzie's 4th Cavalry persuaded them to move to their new, smaller reservation in southwestern Colorado in

---

[157] Roberts, p. 197
[158] Collins, Charles. Apache Nightmare, p. 30.
[159] Lincoln, Annual Report 1881, p. 119.

the summer of 1881. Unrest among the Ute and Navajo could have prevented Pope from shifting troops from Colorado and Fort Wingate west to relieve Fort Apache, leaving Willcox to cope with the uprising there with no more than the troops he had on hand.

While Sherman might vow to send "every available man" to Arizona to suppress the Apaches, the truth is he did not have a lot of soldiers to command. With just 23,596 men in the ranks, the Army was stretched very thin in 1881. Worse, that force included just 6,882 cavalry troopers in 10 regiments spread all over the West. One of those regiments was stationed in the Pacific Northwest; two were in the north watching the Sioux, where Sitting Bull had just crossed the border from Canada and finally surrendered at the end of June; and two regiments were on the Mexican border in Texas. In Arizona, Willcox had just the 6th Cavalry plus two infantry regiments. As commander of the Department of the Missouri, Pope had two cavalry regiments to cover four states and Indian Territory as well as New Mexico Territory.

Nana certainly met with Geronimo and Juh when he visited the reservation in June, and possibly with Naiche, Chatto and Loco as well. It's perhaps significant that none of these or their followers, including the inveterate insurgent Geronimo, volunteered to join the raid. For the Apache, revenge was not just a family duty but a sacred communal obligation. Chatto and Loco had been Victorio's men in the days before the Chihenne were removed to Arizona; Naiche was the son of Victorio's old friend Cochise; Mangas the son of the great Mangas Coloradas. Geronimo was not a Chihenne, but Victorio had allowed him to use Ojo Caliente as a base for his raiding into Mexico in the 1870s, an important factor in the Indian Bureau's decision to close that agency and move everybody to San Carlos. That in turn ultimately led to Victorio's death in Mexico. So Geronimo owed a debt to Victorio's memory. Plus, Nana was his brother-in-law.

Perhaps he remained in Arizona to fan the smoldering fires of discontent on the reservation while Nana attempted to incite unrest among the Mescalero and Navajo.

"Geronimo was a frequent visitor to the agency that summer, loafing around and not doing much of anything," according to Charles Connell, an American who worked at San Carlos.[160] More than boredom and simple curiosity, it could be Geronimo was covertly observing the white men's routine, estimating their readiness, and noting who came and went.

Although years later Jun's son Asa Daklugie was quite definite that his father, Geronimo, Naiche, Chihuahua and Lozen were all involved in the fighting at Cibecue,[161] the military's investigation at the time found no

---

[160] Sweeney, p. 179.
[161] Ball, Indeh, p. 54.

evidence of Chiricahua participation. After personally interviewing two of the White Mountain leaders, Gen. Crook concluded that the outbreak was a spontaneous reaction to Carr's heavy-handed mishandling of the situation.

But Crook was a new broom with no responsibility for these past events, and he needed Apache scouts to penetrate the Sierra Madre. Finding that these potential recruits were disposed to mutinous conspiracy might well have derailed his plans. For their part, the White Mountain leaders were anxious to pin the blame for the Cibecue affray on Carr's provocation. Admitting Chiricahua involvement in the outbreak would have been to confess there had in fact been a widespread conspiracy underway before Carr's military expedition left Fort Apache.

Meanwhile, Willcox and Carr were engaged in a bitter feud over responsibility for the failure to prevent the Chiricahua escape to Mexico. With their careers on the line, neither they nor Agent Tiffany had anything to gain by discovering evidence their charges had been engaged in a plot they should have thwarted before it resulted in bloodshed.

Far better all around to write off the Cibecue mutiny and the subsequent flight of the Chiricahua as an unfortunate misunderstanding.[162]

---

[162] *There are unhappy parallels between the Cibecue affair and*

Tracking Nana

Why did Nana lead his revenge raid into New Mexico? Certainly it was the Americans who drove Victorio over the border, but it was the Mexicans who finally killed him. Visiting fire and death on the people of Chihuahua and Sonora would certainly have more impact on the Mexicans than killing a few ranchers hundreds of miles to the north, and hostages seized locally would have been more valuable than American captives in negotiating for the release of those Chihenne survivors held in Ciudad Chihuahua.

But a raid through New Mexico, reaching to the Mescalero and Navajo reservations, made sense as part of a larger plan. In the summer of 1881, neither Nana nor Geronimo had any intention of fleeing to Mexico. They wanted their own country back, and they still believed they could get it.

If that seems wildly unrealistic in retrospect, it's important to remember that at this point the Apaches had only a dim understanding of the overwhelming power of their American opponents. The railroads had only just arrived in the Southwest, the influx of thousands of settlers was an inexplicable new phenomenon, and the accounts of those few who had actually

the 1993 assault on the Branch Davidian compound in Waco, Texas. In both cases the feds were dealing with a shadowy religious leader they knew little about beyond hearsay and rumor, and in both cases the heavy-handed military response to the perceived threat led to tragedy.

seen the enormous, bustling cities to the east were met with skepticism if not outright disbelief by their fellow tribesmen. From the Apache point of view, they had forced the Americans to draw back once (at the onset of the Civil War), and they had maintained an unstable but survivable stasis with first the Pueblos and then the Spanish and the Mexicans for more than 200 years. In 1881 it would not have seemed impossible to intransigents like Nana and Geronimo that they could yet achieve a similar balance of power with the Americans.

By their stubborn resistance to relocation, the Mescalero had won for themselves a reservation around their sacred mountain in their own home country. Perhaps a victory over the soldiers at Fort Apache could return the Chiricahua to their own sacred spring.

Nana visited first the Mescalero and then the Navajo to recruit volunteers for his own war party. Was he also attempting to incite wider unrest? Perhaps he believed that by his own example, demonstrating that it was possible to fight the whites and win, he could encourage other tribes to resistance. A number of Mescalero and Navajo braves were already off the reservation in the summer of 1881; if more could be induced to take to the mountains they would tie down more of the soldiers.

If there was such an ambitious plot, it collapsed from the outset. Although Carr mishandled his force tactically, the colonel did succeed in fulfilling Tiffany's directive to have the Dreamer "arrested or killed, or both." The loss of their prophet completely demoralized the White Mountain rebels. Without his Power, the dead could not be resurrected – least of all the Dreamer himself.[163] After their attempt on Fort Apache failed, the discouraged insurgents faded into the mountains and depredations around the reservation ended.

Other than the handful who joined Nana in New Mexico, the majority of Mescalero and Navajo warriors refused to be drawn into a wider uprising. The memory of recent defeat was too bitter, and their chiefs reckoned the odds and calculated they had too much to lose in yet another confrontation with the whites.

Finally, Geronimo even failed to unite all the Chiricahua in resistance. Loco and his followers, who constituted a substantial portion if not a majority of the Chihenne at San Carlos, declined to join in the uprising.

Their involvement in the fighting at Cibecue and Fort Apache might explain why Geronimo and Juh were so quick to gather their followers and flee to Mexico in the wake of the failed uprising. As the Bible has it, "the wicked flee when no one is pursuing."[164]

---

[163] *It's significant that a white scout finished off the badly wounded shaman by smashing his head with an ax. Since the Apache believed a man entered the afterlife in the shape he left this plane of existence, this mutilation would have convinced them he could never return.*

Tracking Nana

The scout mutiny and the subsequent flight of the Chiricahua into the Sierra Madre did have one positive result in that it brought Crook back to the Southwest to replace Willcox. Both pragmatic and sympathetic to his Apache opponents, George Crook was probably the one man in the Army who might have averted the disaster overtaking the Chiricahua. Unfortunately he was just one man, and in the end he was powerless to sway the inexorable course of events.

In 1897, a year after Nana's death in Oklahoma, Geronimo dictated a letter to President McKinley that might have served as Nana's last words as well:

> *It is my land, my home, my father's land, to which I now ask to be allowed to return. I want to spend my last days there, and be buried among those mountains. If this could be I might die in peace, feeling that my people, placed in their native homes, would increase in numbers, rather than diminish as at present, and that our name would not become extinct.*

The President never replied, and Geronimo, like Nana, lies buried at Fort Sill.

---

[164] Proverbs, 28:1.

Bibliography:

Ackerly, Neil W. An Overview of the Historic Characteristics of New Mexico's Mines. N.M. Historic Preservation Division, Santa Fe, 1997.

Aleshire, Peter. Cochise: the Life and Times of the Great Apache Chief. New York, 2001.

Aleshire, Peter. Warrior Woman: The Story of Lozen, Apache Warrior and Shaman. New York, 2001.

Anderson, John B. A History of the Mogollon Mining District, New Mexico, UNM Press, 1939.

Bailey, Lynn R. White Apache: The Life and Times of Zebina Nathaniel Streeter, Tucson, Arizona, 2010.

Ball, Eve. In the Days of Victorio; U. of Arizona, 1970.

Ball, Eve. Indeh: an Apache Odyssey; U. of Oklahoma, 1980.

Bardal, Jane. Southwestern New Mexico Mining Towns, Charleston, S.C. 2011

Billington, Monroe Lee. New Mexico's Buffalo Soldiers, U. of Colorado, 1991.

Boddington, Craig, ed. America, The Men and Their Guns That Made Her Great, Los Angeles, 1981.

Bourke, John G. An Apache Campaign in the Sierra Madre, San Carlos, Arizona, 1885.

Bourke, John G. On the Border with Crook, New York, 1891.

Caffey, David L. Chasing the Santa Fe Ring, UNM Press, 2014.

Carter, Forrest. Watch for Me on the Mountain; New York, 1978.

Chamberlain, Kathleen P. Victorio, Apache Warrior and Chief; U. of Oklahoma, 2007.

Chilton, Lance, et al. New Mexico, A New Guide to a Colorful State; UNM Press, 1984.

Tracking Nana

Christiansen, Paige W. The Story of Mining in New Mexico, Socorro, N.M.,1975.

Cleaveland, Agnes Morley. No Life for a Lady, Boston, 1941. (Reprint U. of Nebraska, 1977)

DeWitt, Dave. Avenging Victorio, Los Ranchos de Albuquerque, 2007.

Faulk, Odie B. Crimson Desert, New York, 1974.

Grant, Richard. God's Middle Finger, New York, 2008.

Grinnell, George Bird. The Fighting Cheyennes, New York, 1915 (republished by U. of Oklahoma, 1955)

Hatfield, Shelley Bowen. Chasing Shadows: Indians Along the United States-Mexico Border, 1876-1911. UNM Press, 1998.

Hutton, Paul. The Apache Wars. New York, 2016.

Jameson, Wendell C. Buried Treasures of the American Southwest, Little Rock, Arkansas, 1989.

Journal of Arizona History, Vol. VII, No.3, (autumn 1966)

Julyan, Robert. The Place Names of New Mexico, UNM Press, 1998.

Kenner, Charles L. Buffalo Soldiers and Officers of the Ninth Cavalry, 1867-1898, U. of Oklahoma, 1999.

King, Scottie, ed. "Listen to the Wind; Ghost Towns of New Mexico," N.M. Magazine, Santa Fe, 1978.

Kiser, William S. Dragoons in Apacheland, U. of Oklahoma, 2012.

Kühn, Berndt. Chronicles of War, Tucson, 2014.

Langellier, John. "Honorable Warriors," True West Magazine, July 2012.

Leckie, William H. The Buffalo Soldiers; U. of Oklahoma, 1967.

Lekson, Stephen H. Nana's raid: Apache warfare in southern New Mexico, 1881

Lincoln, Robert T. Annual Report of the Secretary of War for the Year 1881, Vol.I, Washington, 1881.

Looney, Ralph. Haunted Highways: Ghost Towns of New Mexico, New York, 1968.

Lynn, Alvin R. Kit Carson and the First Battle of Adobe Walls; Texas Tech Univ. 2014.

McDermott, John D. A Guide to the Indian Wars of the West; University of Nebraska, 1998.

Meed, Douglas V. They Never Surrendered: Bronco Apaches of the Sierra Madres, 1890-1935. Tucson, 1993.

Michno, Gregory F. Encyclopedia of Indian Wars; Mountain Press Publishing, Missoula, MT, 2003.

Myrick, David F. New Mexico's Railroads; a historical survey, UNM Press, 1990.

Porch, Douglas. Conquest of the Sahara, New York, 1984.

Rakocy, Bill, ed. Ghosts of Kingston Hillsboro, El Paso, 1983

Radbourne, Allan. *"Dutchy: Indian Scout and Apache Raider,"* True West, Nov. 1998, pp. 38-45.

Rickey, Don Jr. Forty Miles a Day on Beans and Hay; U. of Oklahoma, 1963.

Roberts, David. Once They Moved Like The Wind; New York, 1993.

Robinson, Charles M. III. General Crook and the Western Frontier, U. of Oklahoma, 2001.

Robinson, Sherry. El Malpais, Mt. Taylor, and the Zuni Mountains; UNM Press, 1994.

Roland, A.E. "Bob," ed. *"The Ballad of Plácida Romero,"* New Mexico Historical Review, Summer 2011.

Schubert, Frank N. Voices of the Buffalo Soldier; UNM Press, 2003.

Sheridan, Philip H. Record of Engagements with Hostile Indians within the Military Division of the Missouri, from 1868 to 1881. Chicago, 1882.

Sherman, James E & Barbara H. Ghost Towns and Mining Camps of New Mexico, U. of OK, 1975.

Sierra Co Historical Society, History of Sierra County, 1979.

Silva, Lee A. *"Warm Springs Apache Leader Nana,"* Wild West, December 2006.

Simmons, Marc. Massacre on the Lordsburg Road, Texas A&M Univ., 1997.

Sonnichsen, C.L. The Mescalero Apaches, U. of Oklahoma, 1958.

Sturtevant, William C., ed. Handbook of North American Indians, vol 10. Washington D.C., 1979.

Sweeney, Edwin R. From Cochise to Geronimo; U. of Oklahoma, 2010.

Temple, Robert D. Edge Effects, Bloomington, IN, 2008.

Thrapp, Dan. L. The Conquest of Apacheria; U. of Oklahoma, 1967.

Thrapp, Dan L. ed. Dateline Fort Bowie; Charles Fletcher Lummis Reports on an Apache War. U. of Oklahoma, Norman, OK, 1979.

Thrapp, Dan L. Victorio and the Mimbres Apaches; U. of Oklahoma, 1974.

Utley, Robert. Frontier Regulars: The United States Army and the Indians, 1866-1890, New York, 1973.

Utley, Robert. <u>Geronimo.</u> New Haven, Conn., 2012.

Watt, Robert. <u>Apache Tactics 1830-86</u>: Oxford, England, 2012.

Watt, Robert. *"Horses Worn to Mere Shadows,"* <u>N.M. Historical Review</u>, Vol 86, No. 2, Spring 2011.

Wellman, Paul I. <u>Death In The Desert</u>; New York, 1935.

Worcester, Donald E. <u>The Apaches</u>, U. of Oklahoma, 1979.

Made in the
USA
Middletown, DE